COLLECTED WORKS OF RENÉ GUÉNON

THE MULTIPLE STATES
OF THE BEING

RENÉ GUÉNON

THE MULTIPLE
STATES OF THE BEING

Translator
Henry D. Fohr

Editor
Samuel D. Fohr

SOPHIA PERENNIS

HILLSDALE NY

Originally published in French as
Les États multiples de l'être
© Les Éditions de la Maisnie 1932
English translation © Sophia Perennis 2001
First English Edition 2001
Second Impression 2004

Series editor: James R. Wetmore

For information, address:
Sophia Perennis, P.O. Box 611
Hillsdale NY 12529
sophiaperennis.com

Library of Congress Cataloging-in-Publication Data

Guénon, René
[États multiples de l'être. English]
The multiple states of the being / René Guénon ; translated by
Henry D. Fohr ; edited by Samuel D. Fohr — 2nd English ed.

p. cm. — (Collected works of René Guénon)
Includes index.
ISBN 0 900588 59 4 (pbk: alk. paper)
ISBN 0 900588 60 8 (cloth: alk. paper)
1. Ontology. I. Fohr, S.D., 1943– II. Title.
BD312.G813 2001
111—dc21   2001000973

THE PUBLISHER
GIVES SPECIAL THANKS TO
HENRY D. AND JENNIE L. FOHR
FOR MAKING THIS EDITION POSSIBLE

CONTENTS

Editorial Note XIII

Preface 1

1 Infinity and Possibility 7

2 Possibles and Compossibles 13

3 Being and Non-Being 20

4 Foundation of the Theory of the Multiple States 26

5 Relationships of Unity and Multiplicity 31

6 Analogous Considerations drawn from the Study
of the Dream State 35

7 The Possibilities of Individual Consciousness 41

8 Mentality as the Characteristic Element
of Human Individuality 47

9 The Hierarchy of Individual Faculties 53

10 The Limits of the Indefinite 57

11 Principles of Distinction between the States of Being 61

12 The Two Chaoses 66

13 The Spiritual Hierarchies 69

14 Reply to Objections drawn from
the Plurality of Beings 74

15 The Realization of the Being through Knowledge 77

16 Knowledge and Consciousness 81

17 Necessity and Contingency 86

18 The Metaphysical Notion of Freedom 90

Index 97

EDITORIAL NOTE

THE PAST CENTURY HAS WITNESSED an erosion of earlier cultural values as well as a blurring of the distinctive characteristics of the world's traditional civilizations, giving rise to philosophic and moral relativism, multiculturalism, and dangerous fundamentalist reactions. As early as the 1920s, the French metaphysician René Guénon (1886–1951) had diagnosed these tendencies and presented what he believed to be the only possible reconciliation of the legitimate, although apparently conflicting, demands of outward religious forms, 'exoterisms', with their essential core, 'esoterism'. His works are characterized by a foundational critique of the modern world coupled with a call for intellectual reform; a renewed examination of metaphysics, the traditional sciences, and symbolism, with special reference to the ultimate unanimity of all spiritual traditions; and finally, a call to the work of spiritual realization. Despite their wide influence, translation of Guénon's works into English has so far been piecemeal. The *Sophia Perennis* edition is intended to fill the urgent need to present them in a more authoritative and systematic form. A complete list of Guénon's works, given in the order of their original publication in French, follows this note.

The Multiple States of the Being is the companion to, and the completion of, *The Symbolism of the Cross*, which, together with *Man and His Becoming according to the Vedānta*, constitute René Guénon's great trilogy of pure metaphysics. In this work, Guénon offers a masterful explication of the metaphysical order and its multiple manifestations—of the divine hierarchies and what has been called the Great Chain of Being—and in so doing demonstrates how *jñāna*, intellective or intrinsic knowledge of what is, and of That which is Beyond what is, is a Way of Liberation. Guénon the metaphysical social critic, master of arcane symbolism, comparative religionist, researcher of ancient mysteries and secret histories, summoner to spiritual renewal, herald of the end days, disappears here. Reality remains.

Guénon often uses words or expressions set off in 'scare quotes'. To avoid clutter, single quotation marks have been used throughout. As for transliterations, Guénon was more concerned with phonetic fidelity than academic usage. The system adopted here reflects the views of scholars familiar both with the languages and Guénon's writings. Brackets indicate editorial insertions, or, within citations, Guénon's additions. Wherever possible, references have been updated, and English editions substituted.

The present translation is based on the work of Henry Fohr, edited by his son Samuel Fohr. The text was checked for accuracy and further revised by Marie Hansen. For help with selected chapters and proofreading thanks go to John Champoux, and, for final reviews, to John Herlihy and Allan Dewar. A special debt of thanks is owed to Cecil Bethell, who revised and proofread the text at several stages and provided the index, and to Prof. Jocelyn Godwin, who generously put his earlier (1984) translation at our disposal for purposes of comparison. Cover design by Michael Buchino and Gray Henry, based on a drawing of a knot-motif by Guénon's friend and collaborator Ananda K. Coomaraswamy

THE WORKS
OF RENÉ GUÉNON

*Introduction to the Study
of the Hindu Doctrines* (1921)

*Theosophy: History of
a Pseudo-Religion* (1921)

The Spiritist Fallacy (1923)

East and West (1924)

*Man and His Becoming
according to the Vedānta* (1925)

The Esoterism of Dante (1925)

The Crisis of the Modern World
(1927)

The King of the World (1927)

*Spiritual Authority and
Temporal Power* (1929)

The Symbolism of the Cross (1931)

The Multiple States of the Being
(1932)

*The Reign of Quantity and
the Signs of the Times* (1945)

Perspectives on Initiation (1946)

The Great Triad (1946)

*The Metaphysical Principles of
the Infinitesimal Calculus* (1946)

*Initiation and Spiritual
Realization* (1952)

*Insights into Christian
Esoterism* (1954)

Symbols of Sacred Science (1962)

*Studies in Freemasonry
and the Compagnonnage* (1964)

Studies in Hinduism (1966)

*Traditional Forms and Cosmic
Cycles* (1970)

*Insights into Islamic Esoterism
and Taoism* (1973)

Reviews (1973)

Miscellanea (1976)

PREFACE

In our preceding study, *The Symbolism of the Cross*, we set forth a geometrical representation of the being based entirely on the metaphysical theory of the multiple states according to the data furnished by the different traditional doctrines. The present volume will form a sort of complement to the earlier study, for the information given there was perhaps not sufficient to bring out the full range of this altogether fundamental theory; indeed, at that time we had to limit ourselves to what related most directly to the clearly-defined goal we had set ourselves. That is why, setting aside the symbolic representation already described, or at most only referring to it incidentally as need arises, we devote this new work entirely to an ampler development of the theory in question, both—and above all—in its very principles and in certain of its applications as they concern the being more particularly in its human aspect.

Regarding this last point, it is perhaps not useless to recall from the outset that the fact of our pausing to consider matters of this order in no way implies that the human state occupies a privileged rank in the totality of universal Existence, or that it is metaphysically distinguished with respect to other states by the possession of any prerogative whatsoever. In reality, this human state is no more than one state of manifestation among an indefinitude of others; in the hierarchy of the degrees of Existence it is situated in the place assigned to it by its own nature, that is, by the limiting character of the conditions which define it, and this place confers upon it neither absolute superiority nor absolute inferiority. If we must sometimes consider this human state in particular, it is solely because this is the state in which we find ourselves, and it thereby acquires for us, but for us alone, an especial importance; but this is only an altogether relative and contingent point of view belonging to the individuals that we are in our present mode of manifestation. This is why, especially in speaking of superior and inferior states, we always make this hierarchical division from the human point of view, for it is the only term of comparison directly graspable by us as individuals; and we must not forget that every expression is enclosed in a form and necessarily framed in individual mode, so much so that when we wish to speak of anything, even purely metaphysical truths, we can do so only by descending to an altogether different order—an essentially limited and relative one—in order to translate them into the language of human individualities. The reader will doubtless understand without difficulty all the precautions and reservations imposed by the inevitable imperfections of this language, which is so manifestly inadequate to what it must express in such a case; there is an obvious disproportion here, but one found equally in all formal representations whatsoever, including strictly symbolic representations, although these latter are incomparably less narrowly restricted than ordinary language and consequently more apt for the communication of transcendent truths, and so they are invariably used in all truly 'initiatic' and traditional teaching.[1] Indeed, as we have noted time and time again, in order not to alter the truth by a partial, restrictive, or systematized explanation, it is always fitting to reserve a place for the inexpressible, that is to say for what cannot be enclosed in any form and in reality is, metaphysically speaking, the most important thing.

While still considering the human state, if we wish to relate the individual point of view to the metaphysical point of view, as must always be done when it is a question of 'sacred science', and not merely profane knowledge, it can be said that the realization of the total being can be accomplished taking any state at all as a base or point of departure, by reason of the equivalence of all contingent modes of existence when regarded from the standpoint of the Absolute; thus it can be accomplished from the human state as well as from any other, and, as we have said elsewhere, even from any modality of that state, which amounts to saying more particularly

---

1. In this connection it is worth noting in passing that the fact that the philosophical point of view never has recourse to symbolism suffices to show up the exclusively 'profane' and altogether external character of its particular point of view, and of the mode of thought to which it corresponds.

that it is also possible for corporeal and terrestrial man, whatever Westerners may think, led into error as they are about the importance to be attributed to 'corporeity' because of the extraordinary insufficiency of their conceptions concerning the constitution of the human being.[2] Since it is in this state that we presently find ourselves, it is here that we must begin if our goal is to attain metaphysical realization in any degree; and this is the essential reason for considering this case more particularly; but having developed these observations elsewhere, we shall not dwell on them further here, especially since our present exposition will enable us to understand them still better.[3]

On the other hand, to avoid all possible confusion, the reader must be reminded at once that when we speak of the multiple states of the being it is not a question of a multiplicity that is simply numerical, nor even more generally 'quantitative', but rather multiplicity of a 'transcendent' or truly universal order, applicable to all the domains that constitute the different 'worlds' or degrees of Existence considered separately or in their totality, and therefore outside and beyond the special domain of number and even of quantity in all its modes. In fact, quantity—and all the more so number, which is only one of its modes, namely that of discontinuous quantity—is but one of the conditions that determine certain states, ours among them; it could not therefore be transferred to other states, and still less could it be applied to the totality of states, which obviously escapes any such determination. That is why when we speak in this respect of an indefinite multitude, we should always be careful to observe that the indefinitude in question exceeds all number, and also everything to which quantity is more or less directly applicable, such as spatial and temporal indefinitude, which similarly arise only from conditions proper to our world.[4]

Yet another remark is imperative concerning our use of the word 'being' itself, which, strictly speaking, can no longer be applied in its

---

2. See *Man and His Becoming according to the Vedānta* [cited hereafter as *Man and His Becoming*], chap. 23.

3. See *The Symbolism of the Cross*, chaps. 26–28.

4. Ibid., chap. 15.

proper sense to certain states of non-manifestation that lie beyond the degree of pure Being, and which we shall discuss below. However, the very constitution of human language obliges us to retain this same term in such a case for want of a more adequate one, but we attribute to it only the purely analogical and symbolic meaning without which it would be quite impossible to speak in any way of these matters, this providing a very clear example of the insufficiencies of expression to which we have just alluded. In this way, we shall be able, as we have already done elsewhere, to continue speaking of the total being as simultaneously manifested in certain of its states and non-manifested in others, without this in any way implying that for the latter states we must restrict ourselves to the consideration of what corresponds properly to the degree of Being.[5]

In this connection we should recall that to stop at Being and to consider nothing beyond it, as if in some way it were the supreme Principle, the most Universal of all, is one of the characteristic traits of certain ideas found in Western antiquity and the Middle Ages; and while they incontestably contain a metaphysical element not found in modern conceptions, they remain largely incomplete in this respect, and also insofar as they are presented as theories established for their own sakes and not in view of a corresponding effective realization. This, of course, is not to say that there were no other ideas current at that time in the West; we are only referring to those conceptions that are generally known, and whose value and importance have been exaggerated by those who, despite their praiseworthy efforts to react against modern negations, have failed to realize that these are still only fairly exterior points of view, and that in civilizations such as this, where a kind of rift has formed between two orders of instruction superimposed upon each other without ever being opposed, 'exoterism' requires 'esoterism' as its necessary complement. When this esoterism is misunderstood, and the civilization is no longer directly attached to its superior principles by any effective link, it is not long before it loses all its traditional character, for the elements of this order still subsisting in it are like a body abandoned by the spirit, and consequently are henceforth powerless to

---

5. Ibid., chap. 1.

constitute anything more than a sort of empty formalism, which is exactly what has occurred in the modern Western world.[6]

Having provided these few explanations, we can now enter into our subject itself without the delay of further preliminaries, for all that we have already explained elsewhere allows us to dispense with them in great part. We cannot in fact return indefinitely to what we have said in our previous works, for this would be a waste of time; if some repetitions should prove inevitable, we shall try to reduce them to what is strictly indispensable in order to understand what we now propose to set forth, referring the reader when necessary to the appropriate parts of our other works, where he will find complementary discussions or more ample developments of the questions that we must now consider anew. The principal cause of difficulty in this exposition is that all these questions are more or less closely connected to one another, and although it is important to show these connections as often as possible, it is no less important to avoid any appearance of 'systematization', that is, of a limitation incompatible with the very nature of metaphysical doctrine, which, on the contrary, should open up to those who can comprehend and 'assent' to it, possibilities of conception that are not only indefinite in number, but—and we say this with no abuse of language—really infinite, representing the totality of Truth itself.

---

6. See *East and West* and *The Crisis of the Modern World*.

1

INFINITY AND
POSSIBILITY

To UNDERSTAND the doctrine of the multiplicity of the states of the being, it is necessary before considering anything else to return to the most primordial notion of all, that of metaphysical Infinity, envisaged in its relationship with universal Possibility. The Infinite, according to the etymology of the term which designates it, is that which has no limits; and if we are to preserve this word in its strict sense we must rigorously limit its use to the designation of that which has absolutely no limits whatsoever, excluding here every-thing that only escapes from certain particular limiting conditions while remaining subject to other limitations by virtue of its very nature, in which these limitations are essentially inherent—as, from the logical point of view which simply translates in its fashion the point of view that can be called 'ontological', are those elements implicated in the very definition of the things in question. As we have already mentioned on many occasions, these latter include number, space, and time, even in the most general and extended conceptions we can possibly form of them, which far exceed our ordinary notions;[1] all of this can really only be in the domain of the

---

1. It should be observed that we are careful to say 'general' and not 'universal', for here it is nothing more than a question of the particular conditions of certain states of existence, which should suffice to show that there is no question of infinity since these conditions are obviously as limited as the states to which they apply, and which they help to define.

indefinite. It is to this indefinitude, when it is of a quantitative order as in the examples just mentioned, that some people improperly apply the term 'mathematical infinity', as if adding a fixed epithet or qualification to the word 'infinity' did not itself imply a contradiction pure and simple.[2] In fact, this indefinitude, proceeding from the finite of which it is merely an extension or a development (and therefore always reducible to the finite), has no common measure with the true Infinite, any more than an individuality, human or otherwise, even considered with the integrality of the indefinite prolongations of which it is capable, can ever be commensurate with the total being.[3] This formation of the indefinite from the finite, of which we have a very clear example in the production of the series of numbers, is only possible on condition that the finite already contain the indefinite potentially, and even were the limits extended so far as to be lost to sight, so to speak—that is, to the point at which they escape our ordinary means of measurement—they certainly are not abolished thereby; by reason of the very nature of the causal relation it is quite obvious that the 'greater' cannot come from the 'lesser', nor the Infinite from the finite.

It cannot be otherwise when, as in the present case, we consider various orders of particular possibilities that are manifestly limited by the coexistence of other orders of possibilities, and thus limited by virtue of their own nature to such and such determined possibilities and no others, and not to all possibilities without restriction. If it were not so, the coexistence of an indefinitude of other possibilities not included in these, each of which is equally susceptible of an indefinite development, moreover, would be an impossibility and

2. If we sometimes speak of a 'metaphysical Infinite' in order to indicate more precisely that it is by no means a question of the so-called mathematical infinite, or other 'counterfeits of the Infinite' (if we may put it so), such an expression in no way falls under the objection just raised, because the metaphysical order is in fact unlimited, so that it contains no determination but is on the contrary the affirmation of that which surpasses all determination, whereas one who says 'mathematical' thereby restricts the conception in question to a particular and limited domain, that of quantity.

3. See *The Symbolism of the Cross*, chaps. 26 and 30.

thus an absurdity in the logical sense of the word.[4] The Infinite on the contrary, to be truly such, cannot admit of any restriction, which presupposes that it be absolutely unconditioned and undetermined, for every determination, of whatever sort, is necessarily a limitation by the very fact that it must leave something outside of itself, namely all other equally possible determinations. Besides, limitation presents the character of a veritable negation; to set a limit is to deny to that which is limited everything that this limit excludes, and consequently the negation of a limit is properly the negation of a negation, that is to say, logically, and even mathematically, an affirmation, so that in reality the negation of all limit is equivalent to total and absolute affirmation. That which has no limits is that of which nothing can be denied, and is therefore what contains everything, that outside of which there is nothing; and this idea of the Infinite, which is thus the most affirmative of all because it comprehends or embraces all particular affirmations whatsoever, can only be expressed in negative terms by reason of its absolute indetermination. In language, any direct affirmation is in fact necessarily a particular and determined affirmation—the affirmation of something particular—whereas total and absolute affirmation is no particular affirmation to the exclusion of others since it implies them all equally; and from this it should be easy to grasp the very close relation this presents with universal Possibility, which in the same way comprehends all particular possibilities.[5]

The idea of the Infinite we have just presented[6] from the purely metaphysical point of view can be neither discussed nor contested,

4. The absurd, in the logical and mathematical sense, is that which implies contradiction; it is therefore identical with the impossible, for it is the absence of internal contradiction that defines possibility, logically as well as ontologically.

5. On the use of negative terms of which the real meaning, however, is essentially affirmative, see *Introduction to the Study of the Hindu Doctrines*, pt. 2, chap. 8, and *Man and His Becoming*, chap. 15.

6. We do not say 'defined', for it would obviously be contradictory to try to give a definition of the Infinite; and we have shown elsewhere that the metaphysical point of view itself, by reason of its universal and unlimited character, is not susceptible of definition either (*Introduction to the Study of the Hindu Doctrines*, pt. 2, chap. 5).

for by the very fact that it contains nothing negative it cannot contain any contradiction—and this is all the more necessarily so, logically speaking,[7] since it is negation that would occasion contradiction.[8] If in fact one envisages the 'Whole' in the universal and absolute sense, it is evident that it cannot be limited in any way, for it could only be so in virtue of something exterior to it, and if anything were exterior to it, it would not be the 'Whole'. It is important to observe moreover that the 'Whole' in this sense must not in any way be likened to a particular or determined whole, that is, to a totality composed of parts that would stand in a definite relationship to it; properly speaking, it is 'without parts', for these parts would of necessity be relative and finite and so could have no common measure with it, and consequently no relationship with it, which amounts to saying that they would not exist for it,[9] and this suffices to show that one should not try to form any particular conception of it.[10]

What we have just said of the universal Whole in its most absolute indetermination also applies to it when it is envisaged from the point of view of Possibility; and in truth there is no determination

7. We must distinguish this logical necessity, which is the impossibility of a thing's not being or being other than it is—and this independently of any particular condition—from what is called 'physical' necessity or necessity of fact, which is simply the impossibility that beings and things could fail to conform to the laws of the world to which they belong, this latter kind of necessity consequently being subordinate to the conditions by which that world is defined, and which are valid only within the special domain concerned.

8. Some philosophers, having rightly argued against the so-called 'mathematical infinite', and having exposed all the contradictions that this idea implies (contradictions that disappear moreover as soon as one recognizes that here it is only a matter of the indefinite), believe they have also proved thereby the impossibility of the metaphysical Infinite, but all that is proved by this confusion is their total ignorance of what the latter implies.

9. In other words, the finite, even if capable of indefinite extension, is always strictly nil with respect to the Infinite; consequently, neither any thing nor any being can be considered a 'part of the Infinite', this being one of the erroneous conceptions belonging properly to 'pantheism', for the very use of the word 'part' implies the existence of a definite relationship with the whole.

10. Above all one must avoid conceiving of the universal Whole in the fashion of an arithmetical sum obtained by the addition of its parts taken successively, one

here either, or at least only the minimum required to render it actually conceivable to us, and above all expressible to some degree. As we have already had occasion to observe,[11] a limitation of total Possibility is properly speaking an impossibility, since to limit it one would have to conceive it, and what is outside of the possible can be nothing but the impossible; but since an impossibility is a negation pure and simple, a true nothingness, it can obviously not limit anything whatsoever, from which it immediately follows that universal Possibility is necessarily unlimited. We must take great care, however, to understand that this applies only to universal and total Possibility, which is thus only what we could call an aspect of the Infinite, from which it is in no way and in no measure distinct; nothing can be outside the Infinite, for if something were, the infinite would be limited and so no longer the Infinite. The conception of a 'plurality of infinites' is absurd because these 'infinities' would mutually limit each other, and so in reality none of them would be infinite;[12] when we say therefore that universal Possibility is infinite or unlimited, it must be understood that it is nothing other than the Infinite itself envisaged under a certain aspect—insofar as it is permissible to say that there are aspects to the Infinite. Since the Infinite is truly 'without parts', strictly speaking there could be no question of a multiplicity of aspects really and 'distinctively' inhering in it; in fact it is we who conceive the Infinite under this or that aspect because we cannot do otherwise, and even if our conception were not essentially limited—as it is so long as we are in an individual state—it would necessarily have to limit itself, for to become expressible, it must assume a determinate form. What matters is

by one. Besides, even where a particular whole is concerned, there are two cases to be distinguished from one another: a true whole is logically anterior to its parts and independent of them, whereas a whole conceived as logically posterior to its parts, of which it is merely the sum, in fact only constitutes what the Scholastic philosophers called the *ens rationis*, whose existence as a 'whole' depends on the condition of actually being thought of as such. The first case contains in itself a real principle of unity, superior to the multiplicity of its parts, whereas the second has no other unity than that which our thought attributes to it.

11. *The Symbolism of the Cross*, chap. 14.
12. Ibid., chap. 24.

that we should clearly understand whence the limitation comes and on what it depends, so that we attribute it only to our own imperfection, or rather to that of the exterior and interior faculties currently at our disposal as individual beings, which as such effectively possess only a definite and conditioned existence, and do not transfer this imperfection, which is as purely contingent and transitory as are the conditions to which it refers and from which it results, to the unlimited domain of universal Possibility itself.

And, finally, let us add that if one speaks correlatively of the Infinite and Possibility, it is not with the intention of establishing between these terms a distinction which could not in fact exist, but rather because here the Infinite is being envisaged particularly in its active aspect while Possibility is its passive aspect.[13] Now whether we regard it as active or passive, it is always the Infinite which cannot be affected by these contingent points of view, and the determinations, whatever may be the principle by which they are effected, only exist in relation to our own conception. In short, this is what we have elsewhere called 'active perfection' (*Khien*) and 'passive perfection' (*Khouen*), following the terminology of the Far-Eastern doctrine, perfection in its absolute sense being identical with the Infinite understood in all its indetermination; and as we said at the time, this is analogous—though to another degree and from a more universal point of view—to what in Being are called 'essence' and 'substance'.[14] For what follows it must be well understood that Being does not contain the whole of Possibility, and that consequently it can in no wise be identified with the Infinite; this is why we say that our point of view here is far more universal than that from which we envisage Being alone. We mention this only to avoid all confusion, for in what follows we shall have occasion to explain this point more fully.

---

13. These are the *Brahmā* and *Shakti* of Hindu doctrine (see *Man and His Becoming*, chaps. 5 and 10).

14. See *The Symbolism of the Cross*, chap. 24.

2

POSSIBLES
AND COMPOSSIBLES

WE have said that universal Possibility is unlimited, and cannot be anything but unlimited; to wish to conceive of it otherwise is in fact to condemn oneself to being unable to conceive of it at all. This is what makes all modern Western philosophical systems impotent from the metaphysical, that is, the universal, point of view, and this is so precisely to the extent that they are systems, as we have already pointed out on a number of occasions. As such, they are in fact only restricted and closed conceptions, which can have a certain validity in a relative domain by dint of some of their elements but which become dangerous and false as soon as, taken as a whole, they pretend to be something more, and try to pass themselves off as an expression of total reality. It is doubtless always legitimate, should one judge it necessary, to envisage certain orders of possibilities in particular to the exclusion of others, and this is what any science must do; but it is not legitimate to affirm that this is the whole of Possibility, and to deny everything that goes beyond the measure of one's own individual comprehension which is always more or less limited.[1] Yet, to one degree or another, this is the essential characteristic of that systematic form which seems inherent to all modern Western philosophy, and this is one of the reasons why philosophical thought in the ordinary sense of the word does not and cannot

---

1. It is indeed noteworthy that every philosophical system presents itself as being essentially the work of one individual, contrary to the case of the traditional doctrines, where individualities count for nothing.

have anything in common with doctrines of a purely metaphysical order.[2]

Among the philosophers who, by reason of this systematic and truly 'anti-metaphysical' tendency, have tried in one way or another to limit universal Possibility, some, like Leibnitz (whose views, however, are in many respects the least limited), have chosen to make use of the distinction between 'possibles' and 'compossibles'; but it is only too evident that this distinction, to the extent that it is validly applicable, can in no way serve this illusory purpose. Compossibles are in fact nothing but possibilities that are mutually compatible, that is to say whose union in a complex whole introduces no contradictions into the latter; consequently, the 'compossibility' is always essentially relative to the whole in question. Moreover, it is clear that such a whole may be that of the characteristics constituting all the attributes of a particular object, or that of an individual being, or again may be something far more general and extended, such as the totality of all the possibilities subject to certain common conditions forming thereby a certain definite order, say one of the domains included in universal Existence; but in all cases the whole is always determined, for otherwise the distinction would no longer apply. So, taking first an example of a particular and extremely simple order, a 'round square' is an impossibility because the union of the two possibles 'round' and 'square' in the same figure implies contradiction; but these two possibles are nonetheless also realizable, for the existence of a square figure obviously does not preclude the simultaneous existence of a round one in the same space, any more than it does any other conceivable geometrical figure.[3] This may seem too obvious to be worth insisting on, but because of its very

2. See *Introduction to the Study of the Hindu Doctrines*, pt. 2, chap. 8; *Man and His Becoming*, chap. 1; and *The Symbolism of the Cross*, chaps. 1 and 15.

3. Similarly, to take an example of a more extended order, Euclidean and non-Euclidean geometries obviously cannot be applied to one and the same space, but that does not prevent the different modalities of space to which they correspond from coexisting in the integrality of spatial possibility, where each must be realized after its fashion, in accordance with what we will shortly explain about the effective identity of the possible and the real.

simplicity such an example offers the advantage of helping to explain by analogy apparently more complex cases such as the one we are about to discuss.

Now, if instead of a particular object or being we consider what we might call a world in the sense we have already given this word, that is, the entire domain formed by a certain ensemble of compossibles realized in manifestation, then these compossibles must be the totality of possibles that satisfy certain conditions characterizing and precisely defining that world, which constitutes one of the degrees of universal Existence. The other possibles, which are not determined by the same conditions and consequently cannot be part of the same world, are obviously no less realizable for all that, but of course each according to the mode befitting its nature. In other words, every possible has its proper existence as such,[4] and those whose nature implies a realization as ordinarily understood— that is, an existence in any mode of manifestation[5]—cannot lose this characteristic, which is essentially inherent to them, and become unrealizable simply because other possibilities are currently being realized. One can say further that every possibility that is a possibility of manifestation must necessarily be manifested by that very fact, and that, inversely, any possibility that is not to be manifested is a possibility of non-manifestation; expressed thus, it may seem that we are merely defining terms, and yet the preceding affirmation comprises nothing other than a statement of axiomatic truth admitting of no discussion. But if one should ask why all possibilities need not be manifested, that is, why there are at the same time both possibilities of manifestation and possibilities of non-manifestation, it would suffice to answer that the domain of manifestation, being

4. It must be clearly understood that we are not taking the word 'existence' here in its rigorously etymological sense, which strictly speaking applies only to conditioned and contingent being, that is, to manifestation. As we said at the outset, we use the word only in a purely analogical and symbolic way, because in some measure it helps to make understandable what is involved, despite the extreme inadequacy of the word in this context; and we have done the same with the term 'being' itself (see *The Symbolism of the Cross*, chaps. 1 and 2).

5. This is then 'existence' in the proper and strict sense of the word.

limited by the very fact that it is a totality of worlds or conditioned states—an indefinite multitude moreover—could not exhaust universal Possibility in its totality, for it excludes everything unconditioned, that is, precisely what matters most from the metaphysical point of view. As for the question why one possibility rather than another should be manifested, this amounts to asking why it is what it is and not something else, exactly as if one asked why some being is itself and not another, which would certainly be a senseless question. What must be understood in this regard is that a possibility of manifestation does not as such have any superiority over a possibility of non-manifestation; it is not the object of a sort of 'choice' or 'preference',[6] but is only of another nature.

If, concerning compossibles, one should now object that 'there is only one world,' according to the expression of Leibnitz, one of two things follow: either this affirmation is a pure tautology, or it is devoid of sense. Indeed, if by 'world' one understands the whole Universe, or, restricting oneself to the possibilities of manifestation, even the entire domain of all these possibilities, that is, universal Existence, the statement is self-evident, even if its manner of expression is perhaps inappropriate; but if by this term one understands only a certain whole of compossibles, as one usually does, and as we have just done ourselves, it is as absurd to say that its existence prevents the coexistence of other worlds as it would be to maintain that the existence of a circle is incompatible with the coexistence of a square, a triangle, or any other figure (to return to our previous example). All one can say is that just as the characteristics of a determinate object exclude from that object the presence of all other characteristics with which they would be in contradiction, the conditions by which a determinate world is defined likewise exclude from that world those possibles the nature of which does not imply

---

6. Such an idea is metaphysically unjustifiable and can only stem from the intrusion of the 'moral' point of view into a domain with which it has nothing to do; thus the 'principle of the best', to which Leibnitz appeals in this context, is properly speaking anti-metaphysical, as we have already pointed out elsewhere (*The Symbolism of the Cross*, chap. 2).

a realization subject to those same conditions; these possibles are thus outside the limits of the world under consideration, but that in no way excludes them from universal Possibility (since it is a question of hypothetical possibles), nor even, in more restricted cases, from Existence in the proper sense of the term, that is, as comprising the entire domain of universal manifestation. There are multiple modes of existence in the Universe, to one or another of which each possible conforms according to its own nature. To speak of a sort of 'struggle for existence' among the possibles as is sometimes done, and with reference precisely to Leibnitz's conception (while doubtless straying very far from his own thought) certainly has nothing of metaphysics about it, and this attempt to transpose what is merely a biological hypothesis (connected with modern 'evolutionist' theories) is even altogether unintelligible.

The distinction between the possible and the real, upon which many philosophers have placed so much emphasis, thus has no metaphysical validity, for every possible is real in its way, according to the mode befitting its own nature;[7] if it were otherwise there would be possibles that were nothing, and to say that a possible is nothing is a contradiction pure and simple; as we have already said, it is the impossible, and the impossible alone, that is a pure nothing. To deny that there are possibilities of non-manifestation is to wish to limit universal Possibility, whereas to deny that there are different orders among the possibilities of manifestation is to wish to limit it even more narrowly.

Before moving on we should observe that, instead of considering the totality of the conditions that determine a world, as was done in the foregoing, one could also take the same point of view but consider one of these conditions in isolation; for instance, from among

---

7. We mean to say that in metaphysics there is no occasion to envisage the real as constituting an order different from that of the possible, though we must keep in mind that this word 'real' is vague and even equivocal, at least as used in ordinary language and in the sense given it by most philosophers. We made use of it here only because it was necessary in order to dismiss the distinction commonly made between the possible and the real. In what follows we will however give it a much more precise meaning.

the conditions of the corporeal world we might take space, envisaged as what contains spatial possibilities.[8] It is quite evident that by definition only spatial possibilities can be realized in space; but it is no less evident that this does not prevent non-spatial possibilities from being equally realized (and here, restricting ourselves to consideration of the possibilities of manifestation, 'being realized' must be taken as synonymous with 'being manifested') outside of that particular condition of existence which is space. If, however, space were infinite, as some claim, there would be no place in the Universe for any non-spatial possibility, and, logically, thought itself—to take the most common and well-known example—would have to be excluded from existence except on condition of being conceived of as extended, a conception that 'profane' psychology itself recognizes without hesitation as false; but, far from being infinite, space is only one of the possible modes of manifestation, and this latter itself is not at all infinite even taken in the integrality of its extension along with the indefinitude of its modes, each of which is again indefinite.[9] Similar remarks would apply to any other special condition of existence, and what is true of each of these conditions taken separately holds true also for any group of them, of which the union or combination determines a world. Besides, it goes without saying that the several conditions thus united must be mutually compatible, and that their compatibility obviously entails that of the possibles they include respectively, with the restriction that the possibles subject to the given group of conditions can only constitute a part of those which are comprised in each of the conditions envisaged apart from the others, from which it follows that these conditions in their integrality, beyond what they hold in common, will include various prolongations that nevertheless still belong to the same

8. It is important to note that the spatial condition by itself does not suffice to define a body as such; every body is necessarily extended, that is to say subject to space (and consequently susceptible of indefinite division, which points up the absurdity of the atomist conception), but contrary to what Descartes and other advocates of a 'mechanistic' physics have claimed, extension in no way constitutes the whole nature or essence of bodies.

9. See *The Symbolism of the Cross*, chap. 30.

degree of universal Existence. These prolongations of indefinite extension correspond in the cosmic and general order to what, for a particular being, are those of one of its states—for example of one individual state considered integrally, that is, beyond any certain definite modality of that same state, such as the corporeal modality of our human individuality.[10]

10. Ibid., chap. 11; cf. *Man and His Becoming,* chaps. 2 and 12–13.

3

BEING AND
NON-BEING

IN THE PRECEDING CHAPTER we noted the distinction between the possibilities of manifestation and the possibilities of non-manifestation, both being included equally and by the same right in total Possibility. This distinction precedes more particular distinctions, such as those between the different modes of universal manifestation, that is, the different orders of possibilities comprised therein, which are distributed according to the special conditions to which they are respectively subject, and constitute an indefinite multiplicity of worlds, or of degrees of Existence.

If we concede this and define Being in the universal sense as the principle of manifestation, and at the same time as comprising in itself the totality of all the possibilities of manifestation, we must say that Being is not infinite because it does not coincide with total Possibility; and all the more so because Being, as the principle of manifestation, although it does indeed comprise all the possibilities of manifestation, does so only insofar as they are actually manifested. Outside of Being, therefore, are all the rest, that is, all the possibilities of non-manifestation, as well as the possibilities of manifestation themselves insofar as they are in the unmanifested state; and included among these is Being itself, which cannot belong to manifestation since it is the principle thereof, and in consequence is itself unmanifested. For want of any other term, we are obliged to designate all that is thus outside and beyond Being as 'Non-Being', but for us this negative term is in no way a synonym for 'nothingness', as seems to be the case in the language of certain philosophers; besides being directly inspired by the terminology of the metaphysical doctrine of the Far East, it is sufficiently justified by the need to use some kind of terminology in order for one to speak of these things at all; moreover, as we indicated above, the most universal ideas, being the most indeterminate, can only be expressed—to the degree that they are expressible at all—by terms that are in effect negative in form, as we have seen in connection with the Infinite. One can also say that Non-Being, in the sense we have just indicated, is more than Being—or, if one likes, is superior to Being, if one understands thereby that what it comprehends exceeds the extension of Being— and that in principle it contains Being itself. However, when we oppose Non-Being to Being, or even simply differentiate them, it is because neither the one nor the other is infinite, for from this point of view they limit each other in a way: infinity appertains only to the totality of Being and Non-Being, because this totality is identical with universal Possibility.

We can express these things again in the following way: universal Possibility necessarily contains the totality of possibilities, and one can say that Being and Non-Being are its two aspects, Being insofar as it manifests the possibilities (or, more precisely, certain of them), and Non-Being insofar as it does not manifest them. Being, there- fore, contains everything manifested; Non-Being contains every- thing unmanifested, including Being itself; but universal Possibility contains both Being and Non-Being. We would add that non-mani- festation contains both what we may call the unmanifestable, that is, the possibilities of non-manifestation, and the manifestable, that is, the possibilities of manifestation insofar as they are not man- ifested—manifestation obviously containing only the totality of those same possibilities insofar as they are manifested.[1]

Concerning the relations between Being and Non-Being, it is essential to note that the state of manifestation is always transitory and conditioned, and that, even for the possibilities that manifesta- tion includes, the state of non-manifestation alone is absolutely per- manent and unconditioned.[2] And let us add in this connection that

---

1. Cf. ibid., chap. 15.
2. It should be clearly understood that in saying 'transitory' we do not have in view exclusively or even principally temporal succession, which applies only to a special mode of manifestation.

nothing of what is manifested can ever 'be lost', to use a frequently heard expression, other than by its passage into the non-manifested; and of course this very passage (which in the case of individual manifestation is properly a 'transformation' in the etymological sense, that is, passage beyond form) constitutes a 'loss' only from the special point of view of manifestation, for in the state of non-manifestation, on the contrary, all things subsist eternally in principle, independent of all the particular and limiting conditions that characterize this or that mode of manifested existence. All the same, to say truthfully that 'nothing is lost', even with this reservation concerning non-manifestation, one must envisage the totality of universal manifestation, and not simply this or that one of its states to the exclusion of the others, for the continuity of all these states relative to each other always allows passage from one to another without this continual movement, which is only a change of mode (implying a corresponding change in the conditions of existence), being in any way a departure from the domain of manifestation.[3]

As for the possibilities of non-manifestation, they belong essentially to Non-Being and by their very nature cannot enter into the domain of Being, contrary to the situation with the possibilities of manifestation; but as we said above, this implies no superiority of

---

3. On the continuity of the states of the being see *The Symbolism of the Cross*, chaps. 15 and 19. What we have just said should suffice to show that the so-called principles of the 'conservation of matter' and 'conservation of energy', however they may be formulated, are in reality no more than simple physical laws that are altogether relative and approximate, and that, even within the special domain to which they are applicable, they can only hold true under certain definite and restricted conditions, conditions that would persist, *mutatis mutandis*, if one were to extend these laws by a suitable transposition to the whole domain of manifestation. Moreover, physicists are obliged to recognize that in a way it is a question of 'borderline cases' in the sense that such laws would be rigorously applicable only for what they call a 'closed system', that is to say for something that does not and cannot exist, for the reason that it is impossible to realize, or even to conceive of, some whole within manifestation that could be absolutely isolated from all the rest, without communication or exchange of any sort with what is outside of it; such a break in continuity would constitute a veritable gap in manifestation, since from the point of view of everything else that whole would simply not exist.

the one over the other, for both are only different modes of reality and conform to their respective natures. Ultimately, the distinction between Being and Non-Being is purely contingent, for it can only be drawn from the point of view of manifestation, which is itself essentially contingent. This in no way diminishes the importance that this distinction has for us, however, given that in our present state it is not possible for us to place ourselves effectively at a point of view other than this, which remains ours so long as we ourselves are conditioned and individual beings belonging to the domain of manifestation, and which we surpass only through liberating ourselves entirely from the limiting conditions of individual existence by metaphysical realization.

As an example of a possibility of non-manifestation we can cite the void, for such a possibility is conceivable, at least negatively, by excluding certain determinations; the void implies not only the exclusion of every corporeal or material attribute, or even, more generally, of every formal quality, but also of all that pertains to any mode of manifestation whatsoever. It is then nonsense to claim that there could be a void in any state of universal manifestation whatsoever,[4] for the void belongs essentially to the domain of non-manifestation, the term admitting of no other intelligible meaning. We must confine ourselves to these simple remarks concerning the void and not treat the subject exhaustively with all the elaboration this would entail, for that would take us too far afield; and, since serious confusions on the question arise above all concerning space,[5] these related considerations will be more aptly treated in a study we intend to devote particularly to the conditions of corporeal existence.[6] From our present point of view, we must simply add that, however it may be envisaged, the void is not Non-Being but only

---

4. This is what atomists, in particular, claim.

5. The conception of an 'empty space' is contradictory, which, let it be noted, constitutes a sufficient proof of the reality of the element 'ether' (*Ākāsha*), contrary to the theory of various schools in India and Greece, which admit of only four corporeal elements.

6. On the void and its relations with extension, see also *The Symbolism of the Cross*, chap. 4.

what might be called one of its aspects, that is to say one of the possibilities that it contains, which possibilities are other than those included within Being and are therefore outside the latter, even when it is envisaged in its totality; and this shows yet again that Being is not infinite. Besides, when we say that such a possibility constitutes one aspect of Non-Being, this possibility must never be conceived of in distinctive mode, for this mode applies exclusively to manifestation; this explains why, even if we could actually conceive of that possibility which is the void, or any other possibility of the same order, we could only express it in completely negative terms; and this remark, which applies generally to all that relates to Non-Being, further justifies our use of that term.[7]

Such considerations then could be applied to every other possibility of non-manifestation. We could take another example, like silence, but its application would be too simple to be useful; and so we confine ourselves here to adding that just as Non-Being, or the non-manifested, comprehends or envelops Being, or the principle of manifestation, so does silence carry in itself the principle of speech; in other words, just as Unity (Being) is nothing but metaphysical Zero (Non-Being) affirmed, so speech is nothing but silence expressed; but, inversely, metaphysical Zero (Non-Being), while being Unity unaffirmed, is also something more (and even infinitely more), just as silence, which is an aspect thereof in the sense we have just explained, is not merely the spoken word unexpressed, for there must also subsist within it what is inexpressible, that is, what is not susceptible of manifestation (for expression means manifestation, and even formal manifestation) and so of determination in distinctive mode.[8] The relationship that is thus

---

7. Cf. *Tao Te Ching*, chap. 14.

8. It is the inexpressible (and not, as is commonly believed, the incomprehensible) that was originally designated by the word 'mystery', for the Greek μυστήριον derives from μυειν, which signifies 'to be silent', 'to hold one's peace'. Also connected with the same verbal root *mu* (whence the Latin *mutus*, 'dumb') is the word μῦθος, 'myth', which, before being diverted from its meaning to the point where it merely designates a fantastic story, signified that which, since it could not be expressed directly, could therefore only be suggested by a symbolic representation, whether verbal or figurative moreover.

established between silence (non-manifested) and speech (manifested) shows how it is possible to conceive of possibilities of non-
manifestation that correspond by analogical transposition to certain possibilities of manifestation,[9] without our claiming in any
way, even here, to introduce into Non-Being an actual distinction,
which could find no place therein, since existence in a distinctive
mode (which is existence in the proper sense of the word) is essentially inherent in the conditions of manifestation (distinctive mode
here is not necessarily synonymous in every case with individual
mode, the latter implying especially formal distinction).[10]

9. In the same way, one could envisage darkness in a superior sense, as what is
beyond luminous manifestation, whereas in the inferior and more usual sense it
would be simply the absence or lack of light in the manifest, that is to say something purely negative, the symbolism of the color black having moreover the same
double signification.

10. The two possibilities of non-manifestation that we have envisaged here
could be said to correspond to what in certain schools of Alexandrian Gnosticism
were designated as the 'Abyss' (Βυθός) and the 'Silence' (Σιγή), which are in effect
aspects of Non-Being.

4

FOUNDATION
OF THE THEORY OF
THE MULTIPLE STATES

THE PRECEDING EXPOSITION contains the basis for the theory of
the multiple states in all its universality: if one envisages any being
whatsoever in its totality, it must include, at least virtually, states of
manifestation and states of non-manifestation, for it is only in this
sense that one can truly speak of 'totality', as otherwise one is only
dealing with something incomplete and fragmentary that cannot
truly constitute the total being;[1] and since, as we have said above,
non-manifestation alone possesses the character of absolute permanence, manifestation in its transitory condition draws all its reality
from it; and by this it is evident that Non-Being, far from being
'nothingness', is exactly the opposite, if indeed 'nothingness' could
have an opposite, for this would imply granting it a certain degree
of 'positivity' incompatible with its absolute 'negativity', which is
pure impossibility.[2]

This being so, it follows that it is essentially the states of non-
manifestation that assure the being permanence and identity, for

---

1. As we indicated at the outset, if one wishes to speak of the total being, one
must still speak analogically of 'a being' for lack of another more adequate term at
our disposal, but this expression is not strictly applicable.

2. 'Nothingness' is then not opposed to Being, despite what is commonly said;
it is to Possibility that it would be opposed, if it could really enter as a term into any
opposition—but this is not the case, since nothing can oppose itself to Possibility,
something that should be understood without any difficulty in view of the fact that
Possibility is in reality identical with the Infinite.

aside from these states, that is, taking the being only in its manifested aspect, without reference to its non-manifested principle, this permanence and this identity can only be illusory, since the domain of manifestation is properly the domain of the transitory and multiple, involving continual and indefinite modifications. This being so, one will readily understand what, from the metaphysical point of view, one should think of the supposed unity of the 'self', that is, the individual being so indispensable to Western and profane psychology: on the one hand it is a fragmentary unity, since it refers to a part of the being only, to one of its states taken in isolation and arbitrarily from among an indefinite number of others (and this state, too, is far from being envisaged in its integrality), while on the other hand this unity, even if only considered in reference to this special state, is as relative as possible, since this state is itself composed of an indefinite number of diverse modifications and so has even less reality when abstracted from its transcendent principle (the 'Self' or personality), which alone could truly give it reality by maintaining the identity of a being in permanent mode throughout all these modifications.

The states of non-manifestation are of the domain of Non-Being, and the states of manifestation are of the domain of Being envisaged in its integrality; it could also be said that these latter correspond to the different degrees of Existence, which are nothing other than the different modes of universal manifestation, indefinite in their multiplicity. In order to establish a clear distinction between Being and Existence, we must, as we have already said, consider Being strictly as the very principle of manifestation; universal Existence will then be the integral manifestation of the ensemble of possibilities that Being comprises, and which moreover are all the possibilities of manifestation, implying the effective development of those possibilities in a conditioned mode. Being thus envelops Existence, and is metaphysically more than the latter since it is its principle; Existence is thus not identical with Being, for the latter corresponds to a lesser degree of determination, and consequently to a higher degree of universality.[3]

3. Let us recall again that to 'exist', in the etymological sense of the word (from Latin ex-stare), is properly speaking to be dependent or conditioned; it is then,

Although Existence is essentially unique because Being in itself is one, it nonetheless comprises the indefinite multiplicity of the modes of manifestation, for it contains them all equally by the very fact that they are all equally possible, this possibility implying that each one of them must be realized according to the conditions proper to it. As we have said elsewhere, in connection with this 'unicity of Existence' (in Arabic, *Waḥdat al-wujūd*) as found in the teachings of Islamic esoterism,[4] it follows that Existence comprises in its very 'unicity' an indefinitude of degrees corresponding to all the modes of universal manifestation (which is basically the same thing as Existence itself); and for any being whatsoever envisaged in the entire domain of that Existence, this indefinite multiplicity of degrees of existence implies correlatively a like indefinite multiplicity of possible states of manifestation, each of which must be realized in a determined degree of universal Existence. A state of a being is then the development of a particular possibility contained in such a degree, that degree being defined by the conditions to which the possibility is subject insofar as it is envisaged as realizing itself in the domain of manifestation.[5]

Thus, each state of manifestation of a being corresponds to a degree of Existence, and in addition includes diverse modalities in accordance with the different combinations of conditions to which one and the same general mode of manifestation is susceptible; and finally, each modality comprises in itself an indefinite series of secondary and elementary modifications. If, for example, we consider the being in the particular state of human individuality, the corporeal part of this individuality is only one of its modalities, and this modality is not precisely determined by a single condition but by an ensemble of conditions that delimit its possibilities, these conditions taken in combination defining the perceptible or corporeal

---

finally, not to possess in oneself one's own principle or sufficient reason, which is indeed true of manifestation, as we shall explain further on when we define contingency with more precision.

4. *The Symbolism of the Cross*, chap. 1.

5. This restriction is necessary because, in its non-manifested essence, the same possibility obviously cannot be subject to such conditions.

world.[6] As we have already noted,[7] each of these conditions considered in isolation from the others can extend beyond the domain of that modality, and, whether through its own extension or through its combination with different conditions, can then constitute the domain of other modalities that are part of the same integral individuality. Moreover, each modality must be regarded as susceptible of development in the course of a certain cycle of manifestation, and, for the corporeal modality in particular, the secondary modifications that this development includes will be all the moments of its existence (envisaged under the aspect of temporal succession), or, what comes to the same thing, all the actions and gestures, whatever they may be, that it will carry out in the course of its existence.[8]

It is almost superfluous to stress how little place the individual 'self' occupies in the totality of the being,[9] since even given its entire extension when envisaged in its integrality, and not merely in one particular modality such as the corporeal, it constitutes only one state like the others, among an indefinitude of others. This is so even when one limits one's consideration to the states of manifestation; and beyond this, the latter are themselves the least important elements in the total being from the metaphysical point of view, for the reasons given above.[10] Among the states of manifestation are

6. It is this that Hindu doctrine designates as the domain of 'gross' manifestation. It is sometimes called the 'physical world', but this expression is equivocal, and even if it can be justified by the modern sense of the word 'physical', which actually applies only to what concerns sensible qualities, we think it better to preserve the ancient etymological meaning (from φύσις, 'nature') for this word, because when understood thus, 'subtle' manifestation is no less 'physical' than gross manifestation, for 'nature', which is properly speaking the domain of 'becoming', is in reality identical to the whole of universal manifestation.

7. The Symbolism of the Cross, chap. 11.

8. Ibid., chap. 12.

9. See ibid., chap. 27.

10. One might say that the 'self', with all the prolongations of which it is susceptible, has incomparably less importance than modern Western psychologists and philosophers attribute to it, although at the same time it contains possibilities of an indefinitely greater extension than they can even suspect (see Man and His Becoming, chap. 2, and also what we have to say below on the possibilities of individual consciousness).

those, apart from human individuality, that can likewise be individual (that is, formal) states, whereas others are non-individual (that is, non-formal), the nature of each being determined, together with its place in the hierarchically organized totality of the being, by the conditions proper to it, for it is always a matter of conditioned states, by the very fact that they are manifested. As for the states of non-manifestation, it is evident that, not being more subject to form than to any other condition of any mode whatsoever of manifested existence, they are essentially extra-individual; we can say that they constitute whatever is truly universal in each being, and therefore that by which each being, in all that it is, is linked to its metaphysical and transcendent principle, a link without which it would have only an altogether contingent and in fact purely illusory existence.

5

RELATIONSHIPS
OF UNITY AND
MULTIPLICITY

In Non-Being there can be no question of a multiplicity of states, since this domain is essentially that of the undifferentiated and even of the unconditioned; the unconditioned cannot be subject to the determinations of the one and of the multiple, and the undifferentiated cannot exist in a distinctive mode. If we nonetheless still speak of states of non-manifestation, it is not to establish thereby a sort of symmetry with the states of manifestation—which would be unjustified and altogether artificial—but because we are forced to introduce a distinction of some kind, lacking which we could not speak of it at all; however, we must be aware that this distinction does not exist in itself, and that it is we who give it its altogether relative existence, since only thus can we envisage what we have called aspects of Non-Being, even as we admit the inadequacy and impropriety of such an expression. In Non-Being there is no multiplicity, and strictly speaking there is no unity either, for Non-Being is metaphysical Zero, to which we are obliged to attach a name if we are to speak of it, and is logically anterior to unity; that is why Hindu doctrine speaks in this regard only of 'non-duality' (*advaita*), which agrees moreover with what we said above on the use of negative forms of expression.

It is essential to note in this connection that metaphysical Zero has no more relation to mathematical zero, which is only the sign for what can be called a negation of quantity, than the true Infinite has to do with the merely indefinite, that is, with quantity that increases or decreases indefinitely;[1] and this absence of relation, if one can so express it, is of exactly the same order in both cases, with the reservation however that metaphysical Zero is only one aspect of the Infinite—at least, we permit ourselves to consider it as such insofar as, in principle, it contains unity and consequently everything else. In fact, primordial unity is nothing other than Zero affirmed; or, in other words, universal Being, which is that unity, is only Non-Being affirmed insofar as such an affirmation is possible. This affirmation is already a first determination, and is the most universal of all definite and therefore conditioned determinations; and this first determination, prior to all manifestation and to all particularization (including the polarization into 'essence' and 'substance', which is the first duality and thus the starting-point of all multiplicity), contains in principle all the other distinctive determinations or affirmations (corresponding to all the possibilities of manifestation), which amounts to saying that unity, as soon as it is affirmed, contains multiplicity in principle, or that it is itself the immediate principle of that multiplicity.[2]

It has frequently been asked to no purpose how multiplicity can proceed from unity, without it having been noticed that the question so put admits of no answer for the simple reason that it is wrongly posed, and in this form does not correspond to any reality;

1. These two, the indefinitely increasing and decreasing, are what in reality correspond to what Pascal so improperly called the 'two infinities' (see *The Symbolism of the Cross*, chap. 29); and it must be stressed that neither of these can in any way lead us out of the quantitative domain.

2. As it is a point that cannot be overstressed, we reiterate that the unity in question here is a metaphysical or 'transcendent' unity, which applies to universal Being as a 'coextensive' attribute, to use the terminology of logicians (although the notion of 'extension' and the correlative one of 'comprehension' are not properly applicable beyond the 'categories', or the most general types, that is, when one passes from the general to the universal), and which, as such, differs essentially from the mathematical or numerical unity which applies only to the quantitative domain; and it is the same for multiplicity, as we have often remarked before. There is only analogy, and not identity, or even similarity, between the metaphysical ideas of which we speak and the corresponding mathematical notions, the designation of the one and the other by a common term expressing in reality no more than this analogy.

multiplicity does not in fact proceed from unity, any more than unity does from metaphysical Zero, or than anything at all does from the universal Whole, or than any possibility can be situated outside the Infinite or outside total Possibility.[3] Multiplicity is included in primordial Unity, and it does not cease to be so by the fact of its development in manifested mode; this multiplicity belongs to the possibilities of manifestation, and cannot be conceived otherwise, for it is manifestation that implies distinctive existence; moreover, since it is a matter of possibilities, it is necessary that they should exist in the manner implied by their own nature. Thus the principle of universal manifestation necessarily contains multiplicity, all the while being one and even being unity in itself; and multiplicity, in all its indefinite developments, realized indefinitely in an indefinitude of directions,[4] proceeds in its entirety from primordial unity in which it remains ever contained, and which cannot in any way be affected or modified by the existence of this multiplicity in itself, for it could obviously not cease to be itself by an effect of its own nature, and it is precisely insofar as it is unity that it essentially implies the multiple possibilities in question. Therefore multiplicity exists in unity itself, and if it does not affect unity, this is because it has only an altogether contingent existence in relation to it; we can even say that as long as we do not relate it to unity in the way we have just done, this existence is purely illusory, for it is unity alone that, being its principle, gives to it all the reality of which it is capable; and, in its turn, unity is not an absolute principle, nor is it self-sufficient unto itself, but draws its own reality from metaphysical Zero.

Being, since it is only the first affirmation, the most primordial determination, is not the supreme principle of all things; it is only,

---

3. This is why we feel that one should avoid as far as possible the use of a term such as 'emanation', which evokes the idea, or rather the false image, of a 'going out' from the Principle.

4. It goes without saying that this word 'directions', borrowed from considerations of spatial possibilities, must be understood symbolically, for in its literal sense it would apply only to a minute portion of the possibilities of manifestation, the sense we give it here conforming moreover to all that we have expounded in *The Symbolism of the Cross*.

we repeat, the principle of manifestation, and we see by this how very much the metaphysical point of view is restricted by those who claim to reduce it to 'ontology' alone, for to abstract it from Non-Being in this way is even to exclude everything that is in fact most truly and most purely metaphysical. Having said this in passing, we will conclude our exposition of the present point with the following: Being is one in itself, and universal Existence, which is the integral manifestation of its possibilities, is consequently one in its essence and in its inmost nature; but neither the unity of Being nor the 'unicity' of Existence excludes the multiplicity of the modes of manifestation, whence the indefinitude of degrees of Existence in the general and cosmic order, and of the states of the being in the order of particular existences.[5] Therefore, the consideration of the multiple states in no way contradicts the unity of Being, any more than it does the 'unicity' of Existence that is based on that unity, since neither the one nor the other is in any way affected by multiplicity; and from this it follows that in the whole domain of Being, the fact of multiplicity, far from contradicting the affirmation of unity or opposing it in any fashion, finds therein its only valid foundation, logically as well as metaphysically.

---

5. We do not say 'individual', because states of non-formal manifestation, which are supra-individual, are included here.

6

ANALOGOUS
CONSIDERATIONS
DRAWN FROM
STUDY OF THE
DREAM STATE

WE now leave the purely metaphysical point of view of the preceding chapter in order to consider the relationships of unity and multiplicity, for we can perhaps better understand the nature of these relationships with the help of some analogical considerations offered by way of example, or rather of 'illustration' so to speak,[1] which will show in what sense and in what measure one can say that the existence of multiplicity is illusory with respect to unity, while of course still possessing such reality as its nature allows. We will draw these more particular considerations from the study of the dream state, which is one of the modalities of the manifestation of the human being corresponding to the subtle (that is, non-corporeal) part of its individuality. In this state the being produces a world that proceeds entirely from itself, and the objects therein consist exclusively of mental images (as opposed to the sensory perceptions of

---

1. Strictly speaking, no example is in fact possible where metaphysical truths are concerned, for these are universal in essence and not susceptible of any particularization, whereas every example is necessarily of a particular order, to one degree or another.

the waking state), that is to say of combinations of ideas clothed in subtle forms that depend substantially on the subtle form of the individual himself, moreover, of which the imaginal objects of a dream are nothing but accidental and secondary modifications.[2]

In the dream state, man is therefore situated in a world imagined entirely by himself,[3] every element of which is consequently drawn from himself, from his own more or less extended individuality (in its extra-corporeal modalities), like so many 'illusory forms' (*māyāvi-rūpa*),[4] this being so even if he possesses no clear and distinct consciousness of it. Whatever may be the interior or exterior starting-point (which may vary widely according to the case) that gives a dream a certain direction, the events that unfold therein can only result from a combination of elements contained at least potentially and as if capable of a certain kind of realization, within the integral comprehension of the individual; and if these elements, which are modifications of the individual, are indefinite in number, the variety of such possible combinations is equally so. A dream should in fact be regarded as a mode of realization for possibilities that, while belonging to the domain of human individuality, are for one reason or another not susceptible of realization in a corporeal mode; such are, for example, the forms of beings belonging to the same world but other than man, forms that the latter possesses virtually in himself by reason of the central position he occupies in that world.[5] These forms obviously cannot be realized by the human being except in the subtle state, and the dream is the most ordinary—one could also say the most normal—of all the means by which he is able to identify himself with other such beings, without in any way ceasing to be himself, as indicated in this Taoist text: 'One night,' said Chuang Tzu,

---

2. See *Man and His Becoming*, chap. 12.

3. The word 'imagined' should be understood here in its most exact sense, since it is indeed the formation of images that is essentially involved in a dream.

4. See *Man and His Becoming*, chap. 10.

5. See *The Symbolism of the Cross*, chap. 2.

I was a butterfly, flitting about and contented with my lot; then I awoke, to find myself Chuang Chou. Which am I really? A butterfly that dreams it is Chuang Chou, or Chuang Chou who imagines that he is a butterfly? Are there two real individuals in my case? Was there a real transformation from one individual to another? Neither the one nor the other: there were two unreal modifications of the unique Being, of the universal norm, in which all beings in all their states are one.[6]

If in the course of his dream the individual takes an active part in the unfolding events that his imaginative faculty creates, that is, if in the dream he plays in it a determined role in the extra-corporeal modality of his being that at the time corresponds to the state of his clearly manifested consciousness, or to what one could call the central zone of that consciousness, one must nonetheless admit that simultaneously he likewise 'plays' all the other roles as well, whether in other modalities, or at the very least in different secondary modifications of the same modality that also belong to his individual consciousness—and if not in the current limited state of manifestation of this consciousness, then at least in some one of its possibilities of manifestation, which, in their totality, include a field of indefinitely greater extent. Naturally all these other roles appear secondary to the one that is principal to the individual, that is, the one in which his current consciousness is directly involved, and since all the elements of the dream exist only through this individual, one can say that they are real only insofar as they participate in his own existence; it is the dreamer himself who realizes them as so many modifications of himself, without ceasing thereby to be himself independently of these modifications, which in no way affect what constitutes the very essence of his individuality. Moreover, if the individual is conscious that he is dreaming, conscious, that is, of the fact that all the events unfolding in this state have only the reality that he himself gives them, he will be entirely unaffected even if in the dream he is simultaneously actor and spectator, and this is so

6. *Chuang Tzu*, chap. 2.

precisely because he will not cease to be a spectator in order to become an actor, the conception and the realization no longer being separated for his individual consciousness when it has reached a stage of development sufficient to embrace synthetically all the present modifications of the individuality. If the situation is otherwise, the same modifications can still be realized, but if the consciousness does not link this realization directly to the conception of which it is an effect, the individual is led to attribute to the dream events a reality exterior to himself, and, in the measure in which he does so, he is subject to an illusion of which the cause lies within himself, an illusion consisting in separating the multiplicity of those events from their immediate principle, that is to say from his own individual unity.[7]

This is a very clear example of a multiplicity existing within a unity, without the latter being affected by it; and even though the unity in question here may only be relative—that of an individual— in relation to that multiplicity, it nonetheless plays a part analogous to that of veritable and primordial unity in relation to universal manifestation. Moreover, we could have taken another example and considered the perceptions of the waking state in this way,[8] but the case we chose has the advantage over it because the conditions peculiar to the dream world in which one is isolated from all the exterior, or supposedly exterior,[9] things that constitute the sensible

7. The same can be said of cases of hallucination, in which the error does not, as is usually maintained, consist in attributing reality to the perceived object—it being obviously impossible to perceive something that does not exist in any way— but in attributing to it a mode of reality other than that which is truly its own, amounting in effect to a confusion between the orders of subtle and corporeal manifestation.

8. Leibnitz defined perception as 'the expression of multiplicity in unity' (*multorum in uno expressio*), which is correct, but only with the reservations we have already indicated on the unity one can rightly attribute to the 'individual substance' (cf. *The Symbolism of the Cross*, chap. 3).

9. By this restriction we do not at all mean to deny the exteriority of sensible objects, which is one consequence of their spatiality, but only to indicate that we do not wish to enter just now upon the question of what degree of reality one should assign to that exteriority.

world, permit no argument. What produces the reality of this dream world is the individual consciousness alone, envisaged in its complete unfolding, in all the possibilities of manifestation that it comprises; moreover, envisaged thus in its entirety, this consciousness contains the dream world in the same way that it contains all the other elements of individual manifestation belonging to any of the modalities contained in the integral extension of individual possibility.

Now it is important to note that when universal manifestation is considered analogically, all that can be said is that, just as the individual consciousness produces the reality of that special world which is composed of all its possible modalities, there is also something that produces the reality of the manifested Universe, but without its being in any way legitimate to equate that 'something' with an individual faculty or a specialized condition of existence, which would be an eminently anthropomorphic and anti-metaphysical conception. Consequently it is neither consciousness nor thought, but rather that something of which consciousness and thought are only particular modes of manifestation; and if there is an indefinitude of such possible modes which can be regarded as so many attributes of universal Being, direct or indirect, analogous in a certain measure to what, for the individual, are the roles played in the dream state by his multiple modalities and modifications, and by which his inmost nature is no longer affected, there is no reason to try to reduce all these attributes to one or to several of them; or at least there can only be one reason, which is none other than that systematic tendency we have already denounced as incompatible with the universality of metaphysics. Whatever the attributes, they are only different aspects of that unique principle which gives reality to all manifestation because it is Being itself; and their diversity exists only from the point of view of differentiated manifestation, not from that of its principle, or of Being in itself, which is the veritable and primordial unity. This is true even of the most universal distinction one can make in Being, that of 'essence' and 'substance', which are like the two poles of all manifestation; and consequently it is so *a fortiori* for all the more particular aspects, which therefore are more contingent and of secondary importance:[10] whatever value they may take on in the eyes of the individual when he envisages them from his particular point of view, properly speaking they are only simple 'accidents' in the Universe.

---

10. We allude here especially to the distinction between 'mind' and 'matter', such as has been put forward in all Western philosophy since Descartes, which seeks to absorb all reality in one or the other, or in both, of these terms, above which it seems incapable of rising (see *Introduction to the Study of the Hindu Doctrines*, pt. 2, chap. 8).

7

THE POSSIBILITIES
OF INDIVIDUAL
CONSCIOUSNESS

THE PRECEDING DISCUSSION of the dream state leads us to make some general remarks concerning the possibilities contained within the limits of human individuality, and more particularly the possibilities of this individual state envisaged under the aspect of consciousness, which constitutes one of its principal characteristics. Here, of course, we do not mean to place ourselves at the psychological point of view, although this latter can be defined precisely by consciousness considered as a characteristic inherent in certain categories of phenomena produced in the human being, or, if one prefers a more pictorial mode of expression, as the 'container' of these same phenomena.[1] The psychologist, moreover, is no more concerned with investigating the profound nature of this consciousness than is the geometrician with the question of the nature of space, which he takes as an incontestable fact, and which he considers simply as the container of all the forms that he studies. Psychology, in other words, need only concern itself with what we may call 'phenomenal consciousness', that is, consciousness considered exclusively in its relations with phenomena, and without asking whether or not this is the expression of something of another order

---

1. Taken literally, the relationship of container to contained is a spatial relationship; but here it should be taken only figuratively, for what is in question is neither extended nor situated in space.

which, by very definition, no longer belongs to the psychological domain.[2]

For us, consciousness is something entirely different from what it is for the psychologist; it does not constitute a particular state of being, and, in any case, is not the only distinctive characteristic of the individual human state; and even in the study of this state, or more precisely of its extra-corporeal modalities, it is not possible for us to admit that everything refers to a point of view more or less similar to that of psychology. Consciousness is more a condition of existence in certain states, but not strictly in the sense in which we speak of the conditions of corporeal existence, for example. It would be more accurate to say that consciousness is a 'raison d'être' for the states in question, however strange this may at first seem, for it is manifestly that by which the individual being participates in universal Intelligence (*Buddhi*, in Hindu doctrine);[3] but naturally in its determined form (as *ahankāra*)[4] it belongs to the individual mental faculty (*manas*), so that in other states the same participation of the being in universal Intelligence may express itself in an entirely different mode. Consciousness, of which we do not claim to give a complete definition here—which would doubtless be of little use[5]— is therefore something particular, whether in the human state or in other individual states more or less analogous to it, and consequently is in no way a universal principle; if it nevertheless constitutes an integral part and a necessary element of universal Existence, it does so only by exactly the same right as do all conditions proper to any states of being whatsoever, and it possesses no more privilege

---

2. From this it follows that psychology has exactly the same character of relativity as any other special and contingent science, whatever some people claim; nor does it have anything to do with metaphysics; furthermore, one must not forget that it is an entirely modern and 'profane' science, unconnected to any traditional knowledge whatsoever.

3. See *Man and His Becoming*, chap. 7.

4. Ibid., chap. 8.

5. Sometimes definitions of things of which everyone has a sufficiently clear notion can appear more complex and obscure than the things themselves, as is the case here.

in this respect than do the states to which it refers with respect to other states.[6]

Despite these essential restrictions, consciousness in the individual human state, like this state itself, is nonetheless capable of indefinite extension; and even in the ordinary man, that is, one who has not especially developed his extra-corporeal modalities, it in fact extends much further than is commonly supposed. It is true that it is generally admitted that our present clear and distinct consciousness is not the whole consciousness, that it constitutes only a certain portion thereof, and that what is excluded may well exceed the former in extent and complexity; but if the psychologists readily recognize the existence of a 'subconscious'—which they sometimes abuse in making of it an all too convenient explanation, indiscriminately attributing to it everything that they are unable to classify among the phenomena they study—they always forget to envisage correlatively a 'superconscious',[7] as if consciousness could not as easily be prolonged above as below, if indeed such relative notions of 'above' and 'below' can have any meaning here, as it seems likely they do, at least from the psychologists' particular point of view. It should be noted, moreover, that in reality both the 'subconscious' and the 'superconscious' are simple prolongations of consciousness itself and can never take us out of its integral domain, and consequently cannot in any way be compared to the 'unconscious', that is, to what is outside of consciousness, but on the contrary must be included in the complete notion of the individual consciousness.

Considered in this way, the individual consciousness suffices to account for everything that takes place mentally in the domain of individuality, without need for recourse to the bizarre hypothesis of

6. On this equivalence of all the states from the point of view of the total being, see *The Symbolism of the Cross*, chap. 27.

7. Some psychologists have actually used this term 'superconscious', by which, however, they mean nothing but the normal clear and distinct state of consciousness as opposed to the 'subconscious', so that it is only a useless neologism. Our understanding of the 'superconscious', on the contrary, is truly symmetrical with the 'subconscious', taking both in relation to the ordinary conscious state, and thus the term is not a useless repetition of any other.

a 'plurality of consciousnesses', which some people have even understood in the sense of a literal 'polypsychism'. It is true that the 'unity of the self', as ordinarily envisaged, is equally illusory, but if this is so, it is precisely because plurality and complexity exist in the very heart of the consciousness, which prolongs itself in modalities some of which may be very distant and obscure, such as those that constitute what might be called 'organic consciousness',[8] as well as most of those manifested in the dream state.

From another point of view, the indefinite extension of consciousness renders completely useless certain strange theories that have surfaced in our time, of which the metaphysical impossibility suffices to refute completely. Here we do not intend to speak only of the more or less 'reincarnationist' hypotheses, and others comparable to them, as implying a similar limitation of universal Possibility, which we have already discussed sufficiently,[9] for what we have in view more particularly is the 'transformist' hypothesis, which in any case has now lost much of the undeserved respect it enjoyed for a time.[10] To explain this point without undue digression, let us observe that the so-called law of the 'parallelism of ontogeny and phylogeny', which is one of the principal postulates of 'transformism', assumes before all else that there really is such a thing as a 'phylogeny', or 'filiation of the species', something that is not a fact but a completely gratuitous hypothesis; the only fact that can be established is that the individual realizes certain organic forms in the course of its embryonic development, and that to realize these forms in this way it has no need to have realized them already in so-called 'successive existences', any more than that it is necessary that the species to which it belongs should have realized them on its behalf in a development in which the individual as such could have

8. See *Man and His Becoming*, chap. 18.

9. *The Spiritist Fallacy*, pt. 2, chap. 6; cf. *The Symbolism of the Cross*, chap. 15.

10. The success of this theory was due in large part to reasons having nothing 'scientific' about them, but which are directly connected with its anti-traditional character; and for the same reasons we can foresee that even when no serious biologist believes it any more, it will nevertheless linger on for a long time in textbooks and popular writings.

had no part. Besides, embryological considerations apart, the concept of the multiple states permits us to envisage all these states as existing simultaneously in one and the same being, and not as traversable only successively in the course of a 'descent' that could pass not only from one being to another but even from one species to another.[11] In one sense, the unity of the species is more real and more essential than that of the individual,[12] which argues against the reality of such a 'descent'; on the contrary, the being that belongs, as an individual, to a determinate species, is nonetheless at the same time independent of that species in its extra-individual states, and, without going too far, can even have links with other species by simple prolongations of its own individuality. For example, as we have already said above, a man who in dream assumes a certain form thereby makes of this form a secondary modality of his own individuality, and consequently realizes it effectively according to the only mode in which this realization is possible for him. From the same point of view, there are also individual prolongations of a somewhat different order, presenting a more organic character; but this would take us outside the bounds of our present subject, and we must limit ourselves to this passing observation.[13] Besides, a more complete and detailed refutation of the 'transformist' theories must above all connect them to the study of the nature of species and their conditions of existence, a study we could not hope to pursue at present; but it is essential to note that the simultaneity of the multiple states suffices to prove the futility of such hypotheses, which are completely untenable when envisaged from the metaphysical point

11. It must be strictly understood that the impossibility of a change of species applies only to true species, which do not necessarily always coincide with the classifications of zoologists and botanists, who wrongly take for distinct species what are in reality only races or varieties of one and the same species.

12. This statement may seem somewhat paradoxical at first sight, but it is sufficiently justified by a consideration of certain plants and so-called lower animals, such as polyps and worms, where it is almost impossible to determine whether one is dealing with one or with several individuals, and to determine the degree to which individuals are really distinct from one another, whereas the limits of the species, on the contrary, are always clearly enough defined.

13. Cf. *The Spiritist Fallacy*, pt. 2, chap. 8.

of view, and of which the lack of a principle necessarily entails factual errors.

We especially stress the simultaneity of the states of the being because even the individual modifications realized in successive mode in the order of manifestation must be conceived as simultaneous in principle, for otherwise their existence can be only purely illusory. Not only is the 'current of forms' in manifestation—always remembering its altogether relative and contingent character—fully compatible with the 'permanent actuality' of all things in non-manifestation, but, if there were no principle of change, the very fact of change would be deprived of all reality.

8

MENTALITY AS THE CHARACTERISTIC ELEMENT OF HUMAN INDIVIDUALITY

WE HAVE SAID THAT CONSCIOUSNESS understood in its most general sense cannot be regarded as strictly proper to the human state as such, capable of characterizing it to the exclusion of all other states; and even in the domain of corporeal manifestation (which represents only a restricted portion of the degree of Existence in which the human being is situated), and of that portion of it that surrounds us most immediately and constitutes terrestrial existence, there are a multitude of beings not belonging to the human species but which nevertheless bear enough similarity to it in many respects to prevent us from supposing them devoid of consciousness, even consciousness understood merely in its ordinary psychological sense. To one degree or another such is the case of all animal species, which moreover obviously bear witness to the possession of consciousness; it took all the blindness of the systematizing spirit to give birth to a theory as contrary to the evidence as that of the Cartesian 'animal-machines'. Perhaps one should go still further and envisage the possibility for the other organic kingdoms, if not for all beings of the corporeal world, of other forms of consciousness that would appear bound more particularly to the condition of life, but this is not important for what we are now proposing to establish.

However, there is assuredly a form of consciousness, among all possible forms, that is properly human, and this determinate form (*ahankāra*, or 'self-consciousness') is inherent in what we term the 'mental' faculty, that is, precisely that 'internal sense' which is designated in Sanskrit by the name *manas*, and which is truly the characteristic of human individuality.[1] This faculty is something altogether special, which, as has been amply explained on other occasions, must be carefully distinguished from pure intellect, which latter, on the contrary, by reason of its universality, must be regarded as existing in all beings and in all states, whatever the modalities through which its existence is manifested; and one should not see in the 'mental' anything beyond what it really is, that is, to use the terminology of logic, a 'specific difference' pure and simple, the possession of which does not itself confer on man any effective superiority over other beings. There can in fact be no question of superiority or inferiority for one being envisaged in relation to others, except in what they possess in common, which implies a difference, not of nature, but only of degree, whereas the 'mental' is precisely what is special in man, what is not held in common with non-human beings, and therefore cannot be the basis of a comparison between the beings concerned. To a certain degree, the human being could doubtless be regarded as superior or inferior to other beings, depending upon the chosen point of view (this superiority or inferiority only being relative moreover), but consideration of the 'mental', as soon as it is introduced as 'difference' into the definition of the human being, can never provide any point of comparison.

To express the same thing again in other terms, we can simply recall the Aristotelian and Scholastic definition of man as a 'rational animal'; if man is defined in this way, and if at the same time reason, or better still, 'rationality', is regarded strictly as that which the medieval logicians called a *differentia animalis*, it is evident that the

---

1. See *Man and His Becoming*, chap. 8. We use the term 'mental' in preference to any other because its root is the same as that of the Sanskrit *manas*, which is found also in Latin *mens*, English *mind*, and so forth; besides, the numerous linguistic comparisons that one can easily make on the subject of this root *man* or *men*, and the diverse significations of the words formed from it, show that an element regarded as essentially characteristic of the human being is involved here, since it is often used to designate the latter, implying that the being is sufficiently defined by the presence of the element in question (cf. ibid., chap. 1).

presence of the latter cannot constitute anything but a simple distinctive characteristic. In fact, this difference only applies in the animal genus, where it characterizes the human species by distinguishing it essentially from all other species of that same genus; but it does not apply to beings not belonging to this genus, so that such beings—the angels, for example—can in no case be called 'rational'; and this distinction implies only that their nature is different from that of man, without of course implying for them any inferiority in respect of the latter.[2] It should also be understood that the definition just recalled applies to man only as an individual being, for only as such can he be regarded as belonging to the animal genus;[3] and it is indeed as an individual being that man is in fact characterized by reason, or rather by the 'mental', including in this more extensive term reason properly speaking, which is one of its aspects, and doubtless the principal one.

When we say, in speaking of the 'mental' or of reason, or, which amounts to the same thing, of thought considered in its human mode, that they are individual faculties, these should naturally not be understood as faculties that would be proper to one individual to the exclusion of others, or that would be essentially and radically different in each individual (which, moreover, would come to the same thing, for one could not then truly say that they were the same faculties, without the equivalence being merely verbal), but rather faculties that belong to individuals as such, which would have no raison d'être if they were considered aside from a certain individual state and the particular considerations defining existence in that state. It is in this sense that reason, for example, is properly an individual human faculty, for if in the final analysis it is true that in its essence it is common to all men (for otherwise it would obviously not serve to define human nature), and that it differs from

2. We shall see further on that the 'angelic' states are properly the supra-individual states of manifestation, that is, those pertaining to non-formal manifestation.

3. We recall that the species is essentially of the order of individual manifestation, that it is strictly immanent at a certain definite degree of universal Existence, and that in consequence the being is tied to it only in its state corresponding to that degree.

one individual to another only in its application and its secondary modalities, it nonetheless belongs to men as individuals, and only as individuals, precisely because it is a characteristic of human individuality; and one must beware of envisaging its correspondence with the universal in any way but by purely analogical transposition. Thus—and we emphasize this to avoid all possibility of confusion, a confusion the 'rationalist' conceptions of the modern West render all too easy—if one takes the word 'reason' both in a universal and an individual sense, one must always be mindful that this double usage of one and the same term, which, strictly speaking, it would be preferable to avoid, is only the indication of a simple analogy, expressing the refraction of a universal principle (*Buddhi*) in the human mental order.[4] It is only by virtue of this analogy, which is to no degree an identification, that in a certain sense, and with the preceding reservations, one can give the name 'reason' to what in the universal corresponds, by an appropriate transposition, to human reason, or, in other words, to that of which the latter is the expression, as translation and manifestation, in individualized mode.[5] Besides, the fundamental principles of knowledge, even if one regards them as a sort of 'universal reason', understood in the sense of the Platonic and Alexandrian *Logos*, nonetheless surpass all assignable measure, the particular domain of individual reason, which is exclusively a faculty of distinctive and discursive knowledge,[6] on which they impose themselves as givens of a transcendent

4. In the cosmic order, the corresponding refraction of the same principle has its expression in the *Manu* of the Hindu tradition (see *Introduction to the Study of the Hindu Doctrines*, pt. 3, chap. 5, and *Man and His Becoming*, chap. 4)

5. According to the Scholastic philosophers, a transposition of this kind must be effected whenever one passes from attributes of created beings to divine attributes, so that it is only analogically that the same terms can be applied to the one and the other, and then simply to indicate that in God is the principle of all the qualities found in man or in any other being—on condition of course that it is a matter of truly positive qualities, and not of those that, being the consequence of privation or limitation, have only a purely negative existence (whatever may be the appearances), and are consequently devoid of principle.

6. Discursive knowledge, as opposed to intuitive knowledge, is fundamentally synonymous with indirect and mediate knowledge; it is therefore only a very relative knowledge, gained in a way by reflection or by participation. By reason of this

order necessarily conditioning all mental activity. This is evident moreover from the moment one observes that these principles do not presuppose any particular existence but, on the contrary, are logically presupposed as the premises, at least implicit, of all true affirmations of a contingent order. One may even say that by reason of their universality these principles, which dominate all possible logic, have at the same time—or rather, before all else—a significance that extends far beyond the domain of logic, for this latter, at least in its usual and philosophical sense,[7] is and can only be a more or less conscious application of universal principles to the particular conditions of individual human understanding.[8]

Although these few points depart slightly from the principal subject of our study, they seemed necessary in order to explain in what sense we say that the 'mental' is a faculty or a property of the individual as such, and that this property represents the element that essentially characterizes the human state. Moreover, when we speak of 'faculties', we intentionally leave this term with a rather vague and indeterminate meaning, for thus it is susceptible of a more general application in cases where there would be no advantage in replacing it by some other term that is more special because more clearly defined.

As for the essential distinction of the 'mental' from pure intellect, we will only recall the following: in the passage from universal to individual, intellect produces consciousness, but consciousness, being of the individual order, is in no way identical with the intellectual principle itself, although it does proceed immediately from it as the result of the intersection of this principle with the particular domain of certain conditions of existence by which the individuality

character of exteriority, which allows the duality of subject and object to subsist, it cannot find within itself the guarantee of its truth, but must receive it from principles that surpass it, and which are of the order of intuitive knowledge, that is to say purely intellectual knowledge.

7. We make this reservation because, in Eastern civilizations such as those of India and China, logic presents a different character, which makes of it a 'point of view' (*darshana*) of the total doctrine, and a veritable 'traditional science' (see *Introduction to the Study of the Hindu Doctrines*, pt. 3, chap. 9).

8. See *The Symbolism of the Cross*, chap. 17.

under consideration is defined.[9] On the other hand, individual thought, which, according to what has just been said, includes reason along with memory and imagination, is formal and belongs exclusively to the mental faculty united directly to consciousness; in no way is it inherent in the transcendent intellect (*Buddhi*), whose attributes are essentially non-formal.[10] This clearly shows to what degree this mental faculty is really something limited and specialized, while nonetheless remaining capable of unfolding indefinite possibilities; it is thus both much less and much more than it appears in the simplified, and even 'simplistic', conceptions current among Western psychologists.[11]

9. As we have explained elsewhere, this intersection is that of the 'Celestial Ray' with its plane of reflection (ibid., chap. 24).

10. See *Man and His Becoming*, chaps. 7 and 8.

11. This is the same observation that we made above on the subject of the possibilities of the 'self' and of its place in the total being.

9

THE HIERARCHY
OF INDIVIDUAL
FACULTIES

As we have just said, the profound distinction between the intellect and mentality consists essentially in the fact that the first is of the universal order, whereas the second is of the purely individual order; consequently, they cannot apply to the same domain or to the same objects, and in this respect there is good reason to distinguish the non-formal idea from the formal thought that is only its mental expression, that is, its translation into individual mode. The being's activity in these two different orders, intellectual and mental, can become so dissociated as to make them completely independent of each other as far as their respective manifestations are concerned even while being exercised simultaneously; but we mention this only in passing, since further development of this subject would inevitably require that we forsake the strictly theoretical point of view to which we intend to limit ourselves at present.

Moreover, the psychic principle that characterizes human individuality is also dual in nature: apart from the mental element properly speaking, it also includes the sentimental or emotive element, which obviously belongs to the domain of individual consciousness as well, but is even further removed from the intellect while at the same time being more closely dependent on organic conditions, thus closer to the corporeal or sensible world. This new distinction, although established within the strictly individual domain and hence less fundamental than the preceding, is nevertheless far more profound than might be supposed at first sight; and many errors or misapprehensions of Western philosophy, particularly under its psychological form,[1] arise from the fact that, despite appearances, it is fundamentally no more aware of this distinction than it is of the distinction between intellect and mentality, or at least it fails to recognize its real significance. What is more, the distinction, and we could even say the separation, of these faculties shows that there is a veritable multiplicity of states, or more precisely of modalities, in the individual himself, although in his totality the individual constitutes only a single state of the total being; the analogy of the part to the whole is found here, as everywhere.[2] One can therefore speak of a hierarchy of individual faculties as well as of a hierarchy of the states of the total being, but the faculties of the individual, although they may be indefinite in their possible extension, are definite in number, and the simple fact of subdividing them to a greater or lesser extent by a dissociation pushed to one or another degree, obviously adds to them no new potentiality, whereas, as we have already said, the states of the being are truly indefinite in their multiplicity, since by their very nature they correspond to all the degrees of universal Existence, at least for the manifested states. One could say that in the individual order the distinction operates only by division, whereas in the extra-individual order, on the contrary, it operates by multiplication, the analogy operating here, as in all cases, in an inverse sense.[3]

We have no intention of entering here upon a specialized and detailed study of the different individual faculties and their respective functions or attributes. Such a study would necessarily have a psychological character, at least as long as we confined ourselves to the theory of these faculties, which in any case need only be named

---

1. We use this expression deliberately, since there are some who, instead of giving to psychology its legitimate place as a specialized science, try to make it the point of departure for, and the foundation of a whole pseudo-metaphysics, which, needless to say, is worthless.

2. See *The Symbolism of the Cross*, chaps. 2 and 3.

3. Ibid., chaps. 2 and 29.

for their proper objects to be clearly enough defined—provided of course that we keep to generalities, our sole concern just now. Since the more or less subtle analyses of this kind are not the province of metaphysics, and since usually they are the more futile, the more subtle they are, we gladly abandon them to those philosophers who profess to enjoy such things; our present intention on the contrary is not to treat the constitution of the human being completely, which we have already done in another work;[4] and this relieves us of the need to develop more fully such points which are of secondary importance in relation to the subject that now occupies us.

In short, if we have seen fit to say a few words on the hierarchy of the individual faculties, it is only because in so doing we can better understand what the multiple states are by giving a sort of reduced image of them insofar as they are comprised within the limits of individual human possibility. This image can only be exact in its own frame of reference if one takes into account the reservations we made concerning the application of analogy; furthermore, since the less restricted it is the more useful it will be, it seems fitting to include, along with the general notion of the hierarchy of the faculties, a consideration of the various prolongations of the individuality already discussed above. These prolongations, moreover, which are of different orders, can be included among the subdivisions of the general hierarchy; there are even some which, as we have said, are in a way organic in nature and simply relate to the corporeal order, but on condition that we see even in the latter something psychic to a certain degree, this corporeal manifestation being as it were enveloped and permeated at the same time by the subtle manifestation, in which it has its immediate principle. In truth, there is no reason to separate the corporeal much more profoundly from other individual orders, that is, from other modalities belonging to the same individual state envisaged in the integrality of its extension, than the latter must be separated among themselves, since it is situated on the same level as they in the totality of universal Existence, and consequently in the totality of the states of the being; but,

4. *Man and His Becoming.*

whereas the others were neglected or forgotten, this distinction has taken on an exaggerated importance by reason of the 'mind–matter' dualism that has for various reasons prevailed in the philosophical tendencies of the entire modern West.[5]

5. See *Introduction to the Study of the Hindu Doctrines*, pt. 2, chap. 8; and *Man and His Becoming*, chap. 5. As we have already indicated, it is principally to Descartes that one must trace the origin of and the responsibility for this dualism, although it must also be recognized that his concepts owed their success to the fact that they were in effect only the systematization of pre-existing tendencies, the very tendencies that are properly characteristic of the modern spirit (cf. *The Crisis of the Modern World*, chap. 4).

10

THE LIMITS OF
THE INDEFINITE

ALTHOUGH WE HAVE SPOKEN of a hierarchy of the individual faculties, it is important never to lose sight of the fact that they are all contained in the extension of one and the same state of the total being, that is to say in a horizontal plane of the geometrical representation of the being such as we expounded in our earlier study [*The Symbolism of the Cross*], whereas the hierarchy of the different states is represented by their superposition in the direction of the vertical axis of the same representation. Properly speaking, then, the first of these two hierarchies cannot be said to occupy any place in the second, since its totality is there reduced to one single point (that of the intersection of the vertical axis with the plane corresponding to the state under consideration); in other words, the differences among individual modalities, having to do only with 'amplitude', are strictly nil in the direction of 'exaltation'.[1]

It should not be forgotten however that in the integral unfolding of the being, 'amplitude' is no less indefinite than 'exaltation'; and it is this that allows one to speak of the indefinitude of possibilities in each state, without of course suggesting that this indefinitude should be interpreted in any way as supposing an absence of limits. We have already sufficiently explained this in establishing the distinction between the Infinite and the indefinite, but here we can

---

1. On the significance of these terms borrowed from Islamic esoterism, see *The Symbolism of the Cross*, chap. 3.

introduce a geometrical figure we have not yet mentioned: in any horizontal plane, the limits of the indefinite are marked by the delimiting circle to which certain mathematicians have given the absurd name of the 'infinite straight line',[2] and this circle is not closed at any point, being a great circle (the section of a diametrical plane) of the indefinite spheroid of which the deployment comprehends the whole of extension representing the totality of the being.[3] If we now consider the individual modifications in their own plane as parts of any cycle exterior to the center (that is, without identification with the latter by way of the centripetal radius), which cycle propagates itself indefinitely in a vibratory mode, the arrival of these modifications at the limit of the circle following the centrifugal radius corresponds to their maximum dispersion, while at the same time necessarily being the stopping-point of their centrifugal movement. This movement, indefinite in every direction, represents the multiplicity of partial points of view outside the unity of the central point of view, from which latter, however, they all proceed like radii emanating from a common center, and which thus constitutes their essential and fundamental unity, although one that is not yet actually realized from the standpoint of their gradual, contingent, and multiform exteriorization in the indefinitude of manifestation.

Here we speak of exteriorization, placing ourselves at the point of view of manifestation itself, but it should not be forgotten that all exteriorization as such is essentially illusory since, as we said above, multiplicity, which is contained within unity without the latter's being affected thereby, can never really emerge from it, for that would imply an 'alteration' (in the etymological sense) in contradiction to principial immutability.[4] The indefinite multitude of partial

2. This term is derived from the fact that a circle whose radius increases indefinitely has for its limit a straight line; and in analytical geometry the equation of this limit of the circle, which is the locus of all points on any given plane that are indefinitely distant from the center (that is, the origin of the coordinates), is effectively reduced to a first-degree equation, like that of a straight line.

3. See *The Symbolism of the Cross*, chap. 20.

4. On the distinction between the 'interior' and 'exterior', and the limits within which it is valid, see *The Symbolism of the Cross*, chap. 29.

points of view, which are all the modalities of a being in each one of
its states, are in their entirety only fragmentary aspects of the central point of view (the fragmentation also being altogether illusory,
since this point of view is in reality indivisible by the very fact that
unity is without parts), and their 'reintegration' into the unity of
this central and principial point of view is properly only an 'integra-
tion' in the mathematical sense of the term: it does not mean that at
some moment the elements could ever have been truly detached
from their sum-total, or ever be so considered other than by simple
abstraction. It is true that this abstraction is not always effected
consciously, since it is a necessary consequence of the restriction of
the individual faculties under one or another of their special modalities, modalities that can only be actually realized by the being that
is placed at one or another of the partial points of view in question
here.

These few remarks may help us understand how one must envisage the limits of the indefinite, and how their realization is an
important factor in the effective unification of the being.[5] Moreover, it is fitting to recognize that to conceive of them, even in a simply theoretical manner, cannot be achieved without some difficulty;
and this is perfectly normal, since the indefinite is precisely that of
which the limits keep receding until lost to sight, that is to say until
they exceed the reach of our faculties, at least in their normal usage;
but since these faculties are themselves susceptible of an indefinite
extension, it is not in virtue of their nature itself that the indefinite
surpasses them, but only in virtue of a limitation of fact due to the
present degree of development of most human beings, so that there
is no impossibility in this conception, which, moreover, could not
take us outside the order of individual possibilities. However that
may be, greater precision on this question would require more particular consideration of the special conditions of one definite state
of existence, for example, or, to speak more strictly, of one definite
modality, such as that which constitutes corporeal existence, but

5. This should be compared with what we have said elsewhere: that it is in the
plenitude of expansion that perfect homogeneity is achieved, just as, inversely,
extreme distinction is only realizable in extreme universality (ibid., chap. 20).

this we cannot do within the scope of the present study. On this matter we once again refer the reader to the study we propose to devote entirely to this subject of the conditions of corporeal existence.[6]

---

6. Guénon commenced a study entitled 'The Conditions of Corporeal Existence' in the January and February 1912 issues of the journal *La Gnose*; unfortunately, this journal then ceased publication, and the study was not continued. The material that did appear is now contained in *Miscellanea*, pt 2, chap. 4. ED.

11

PRINCIPLES OF
DISTINCTION BETWEEN
THE STATES OF BEING

UP TO THIS POINT, in what has more particularly concerned the human being, we have above all considered the extension of individual possibility, which alone constitutes the properly human state; but the being that possesses this state also possesses all the other states, at least virtually, for without them there could be no question of the total being. If one considers all these states in their relation to the individual human state, one can class them as 'pre-human' and 'post-human', but without thereby suggesting any idea of temporal succession, there being no question here of 'before' or 'after' except in an altogether symbolic sense.[1] In the various cycles of the being's development, the order of consequence is purely logical, or rather both logical and ontological, since metaphysically, that is to say from the principial point of view, all these cycles are essentially simultaneous and can only become successive accidentally, as it were, with regard to certain special conditions of manifestation.

---

1. Cf. *Man and His Becoming*, chap. 17. This temporal symbolism, moreover, is constantly used in the theory of cycles, whether the latter be applied to the totality of beings or to each being in particular. Cosmic cycles are nothing other than the states or degrees of universal Existence, or, in the case of subordinate or more restricted cycles, their secondary modalities; moreover, by virtue of the analogy of the part to the whole, which we have already mentioned, the subordinate cycles represent phases corresponding to those of the more extended cycles in which they are integrated.

We must once again emphasize that the temporal condition, conceived in however generalized a way, is applicable only to certain cycles or to certain particular states such as the human, or even only to certain modalities of these states, such as the corporeal modality (certain of the prolongations of the human individuality being capable of escaping time, without thereby leaving the order of individual possibilities), and can in no way intervene in the totalization of the being.[2] It is exactly the same in the case of the spatial condition, moreover, or of any other condition to which we are currently subject as individual beings, as well as of those conditions to which all the other states of manifestation included in the whole of the domain of universal Existence are subject.

It is assuredly legitimate to establish a distinction within the totality of the states of the being by relating them to the human state (as we have just done), whether one calls them logically anterior and posterior, or even superior or inferior to this state, and from the outset we have given reasons that justify such a distinction; but in truth this is only a very particular point of view, and the fact that it is currently ours should not give us any illusions in this regard; in addition, in all cases where it is not indispensable to place oneself at this point of view, it is better to have recourse to a principle of distinction of a more general order and which presents a more fundamental character, without, however, forgetting that all distinction is necessarily contingent. The most principial distinction of all, if one may put it so, and the one susceptible of the most universal application, is that which divides the states of manifestation from the states of non-manifestation, which, because it is of capital importance for the whole theory of the multiple states, we actually posed before any other at the beginning of the present study. Nevertheless, one sometimes has occasion to envisage more restricted distinctions. One such example is the distinction one could establish when one is no

---

2. This is true not only of time but even of 'duration', envisaged, according to certain conceptions, as comprehending, besides time, all other possible modes of succession, that is to say all the conditions that in other states of existence correspond analogically to what is time in the human state (see *The Symbolism of the Cross*, chap. 30).

longer referring to universal manifestation in its integrality, but simply to one or another of the general or special conditions of existence known to us; one could also divide the states of being into two categories, according to whether or not they were subject to the condition in question, and in all cases the states of non-manifestation, being unconditioned, will necessarily belong to the second category, of which the determination is purely negative. Thus, we will have on the one hand the states included within a certain determined domain of greater or lesser extension, and on the other hand all the rest, that is, all the states that lie outside this same domain; there will consequently be a certain asymmetry and a sort of disproportion between these two categories, of which only the first is delimited in reality, whatever may be the characteristic element serving to determine it.[3] To represent this geometrically, one could consider any closed curve traced on a plane as dividing the whole plane into two regions, one situated inside the curve, which envelops and defines it, and the other extending to everything lying outside that same curve; the first of these regions will be definite, the second indefinite. The same considerations apply to a closed surface within the three-dimensional extension which we have taken to symbolize the totality of the being; but it is important to note that in this case, too, one of the regions is strictly defined as soon as the surface is closed, although it nonetheless contains an indefinitude of points, whereas, in the division of the states of the being, the category susceptible of a positive determination and thus of an effective delimitation nevertheless comprises possibilities of indefinite development, however restricted one may suppose this to be in relation to the totality. To obviate this imperfection in the geometrical representation, one need only remove the restriction we imposed by considering a closed surface to the exclusion of an open one: any line or surface whatsoever, in approaching the limits of the indefinite, is in effect always reducible to a closed curve or surface,[4] so that one can say

---

3. Cf. *Man and His Becoming*, chap. 2.

4. Thus it is, for example, that the straight line is reducible to a circumference and the plane to a sphere, as their respective limits, when their radii are taken as projected indefinitely.

that it divides the plane or the volume into two regions, both of which can be indefinite in extension, but only one of which, as in the preceding, is conditioned by a positive determination resulting from the properties of the curve or surface under consideration.

In the case where one establishes a distinction by relating the totality of states to any single state, whether human or any other, the determining principle is of an order different from the one we have just indicated, for it is no longer reducible purely and simply to the affirmation and negation of a certain condition.[5] Geometrically, one must then consider the volume as divided in two by the plane representing the state taken as a basis or term of comparison, what is situated on either side of the envisaged plane then presenting a sort of symmetry or equivalence lacking in the previous case. This is the distinction that we have set forth elsewhere, in its most general form, in connection with the Hindu theory of the three *gunas*;[6] the plane serving as a basis is in principle indeterminate, and can represent any conditioned state whatsoever, so that it is only secondarily, when choosing to place oneself at the point of view of that particular state, that one may define it as representing the human state.

Furthermore, to facilitate correct applications of this analogy, it may be advantageous to extend the last representation to all cases, even to those to which it does not seem directly suitable, given the preceding considerations. To this end we need only envisage the base plane as that by which one determines the distinction in question, whatever may be its principle; the extended part lying below this plane will represent what is subject to the determination concerned, while the part above will then represent what is not subject to that same determination. The only drawback in such a representation is that the two regions of the overall extension seem to be equally indefinite, and indefinite in the same way; but one can efface this symmetry by regarding their plane of separation as the

---

5. It should be clear moreover that it is the negation of a condition, that is, of a determination or a limitation, that has a positive character from the point of view of absolute reality, as we have explained in connection with the use of terms of negative form.

6. *The Symbolism of the Cross*, chap. 5.

limit of a sphere of which the center is indefinitely distant in a downward direction, which in reality brings us back to the first mode of representation, for this is only a particular instance of that reduction to a closed surface to which we have just alluded. In sum, it suffices to keep in mind that the appearance of symmetry in such a case is only due to a certain imperfection in the symbol employed; moreover, one can always pass from one representation to another when one finds another more convenient or in some way more advantageous, since by very reason of that imperfection, in the nature of things inevitable, as we have often had occasion to point out, any single representation is generally insufficient to fully render a conception of the order concerned here (and this is leaving aside what is inexpressible).

Although the states of being may be divided into two categories in various ways, it goes without saying that in none of these divisions is there any trace whatsoever of dualism, for the division is effected by means of a single principle, such as a certain condition of existence, and thus, in reality, there is only a single determination, but which is envisaged both positively and negatively at the same time. Besides, to dismiss all suspicion of dualism, however unjustified it may be, it suffices to observe that all these distinctions, far from being irreducible, exist only from the very relative point of view through which they are established, and even that they acquire this contingent existence, the only existence of which they are capable, solely in the measure in which we ourselves bestow it by our conception. The point of view of manifestation in its entirety, although obviously more universal than others, like them remains altogether relative, since manifestation itself is purely contingent; and this observation applies even to the distinction we considered between the most fundamental and the closest to the principial order, that between the states of manifestation and non-manifestation, as we already took care to point out when speaking of Being and Non-Being.

12

THE TWO CHAOSES

AMONG the distinctions founded on the consideration of a condition of existence, as set forth in the last chapter, one of the most
important—indeed, we could even say the most important—is the
distinction between the formal and non-formal states, for metaphysically this is nothing other than an aspect of the distinction
between the individual and the universal, the latter being seen to
comprise both non-manifestation and non-formal manifestation,
as we have explained elsewhere.[1] Indeed, form is a particular condition of certain modes of manifestation, and it is as such that it is
notably one of the conditions of existence in the human state; but at
the same time it is generally the mode of limitation that properly
characterizes individual existence, and can serve it as some sort of
definition. However, it must be understood that here form is not
necessarily determined as spatial and temporal, as it is in the particular case of corporeal human modality; in no way can it be so for
non-human states which are not subject to space or time, but rather
to other conditions altogether.[2] Thus, form is a condition common,

---

1. *Man and His Becoming*, chap. 2.
2. Ibid., chap. 19, and also *The Symbolism of the Cross*, chap. 1. 'Form, geometrically speaking, is contour: it is the appearance of the Limit' (Matgioi, *La Voie Metaphysique* [Paris: Éditions Traditionnelles, 1952] p71). It could be defined as an
ensemble of directional tendencies, by analogy with the tangential equation of a
curve, and it goes without saying that this geometrical conception can be transposed into the qualitative order. Let us also point out that such considerations are
also relevant to the non-individualized elements (though not the supra-individual
ones) of the 'intermediary world', to which Far-Eastern tradition gives the generic
name of 'wandering influences', and to their possibility of temporary and transitory
individualization, and of directional determination, by entry into relationship with
a human consciousness (cf. *The Spiritist Fallacy*, pt. 1, chap. 7).

not to all modes of manifestation, but at least to all its individual modes which are differentiated among themselves by the addition of various other more particular conditions; what constitutes the proper nature of an individual as such is being clothed in a form, and everything that belongs to its domain, such as individual thought in man, is equally formal.[3] The distinction we have just called to mind is thus fundamentally that between individual states and both non-individual and supra-individual states, the former comprising in their totality all formal possibilities, and the latter all non-formal possibilities.

The totalities of formal possibilities and of non-formal possibilities are what the various traditional doctrines symbolize by the 'Lower Waters' and the 'Upper Waters' respectively;[4] in a general way and in the most extended sense, the 'Waters' represent Possibility understood as 'passive perfection',[5] or the universal plastic principle, which, in Being, is determined as 'substance' (the potential aspect of Being), this last case referring only to the totality of the possibilities of manifestation, since the possibilities of non-manifestation are beyond Being.[6] The 'surface of the Waters', or their plane of separation, which we have described elsewhere as the plane of reflection of the 'Celestial Ray',[7] therefore marks the state in which the passage from the individual to the universal is operative, and the well-known symbol of 'walking on the Waters' represents emancipation from form, or liberation from the individual condition.[8] The

---

3. It is doubtless in this way that we should understand Aristotle when he says that 'man [as individual] never thinks without images,' that is, without forms.

4. The separation of the Waters, from the cosmogonic point of view, is described at the beginning of Genesis (1:6–7).

5. See *The Symbolism of the Cross*, chap. 23.

6. See *Man and His Becoming*, chap. 5.

7. *The Symbolism of the Cross*, chap. 24. It is also, in Hindu symbolism, the plane by which the *Brahmānda* or 'World Egg', at the center of which lies *Hiranyagarbha*, is divided into halves; this 'World Egg' is moreover often represented as floating on the surface of the primordial Waters (see *Man and His Becoming*, chaps. 5 and 13).

8. *Nārāyana*, which is one of the names of *Vishnu* in the Hindu tradition, signifies literally 'He who walks on the Waters,' the parallel with the Gospel tradition being self-evident. Naturally, the symbolic significance here, as in all cases, does not

being that has attained the state that for it corresponds to the 'surface of the Waters', but without yet having risen above this surface, finds itself as if suspended between two chaoses, in which at first there is only confusion and obscurity (*tamas*), until the moment of illumination that determines its harmonic organization in the passage from potency to act, and which results in the hierarchization that will bring order out of the chaos, as does the cosmogonic *Fiat Lux*.[9]

This consideration of the two chaoses corresponding to the formal and the non-formal, is indispensable for the comprehension of a great number of symbolic and traditional figures,[10] and this is why we have mentioned it especially here. Moreover, although we have already treated this question in our preceding study, it is too closely connected with our present subject for us to fail to mention it again, at least briefly.

---

in any way infringe on the historical character of the latter account, a fact that is the less contestable, moreover, since the event concerned, corresponding to the attainment of a certain degree of effective initiation, is far less rare than is ordinarily supposed.

9. See *The Symbolism of the Cross*, chaps. 24 and 27.

10. Cf. especially the Far-Eastern symbolism of the Dragon, corresponding in a certain way to the Western theological conception of the Word as the 'locus of possibles' (see *Man and His Becoming*, chap. 16).

13

THE SPIRITUAL
HIERARCHIES

ONLY THE HIERARCHIZATION of the multiple states in the effective realization of the total being enables us to understand how, from the point of view of pure metaphysics, one must envisage the 'spiritual hierarchies', as they are generally called. This term is usually understood to mean hierarchies of beings differing from man and from each other, as if each degree were occupied by special beings, respectively limited to corresponding states; but the concept of the multiple states manifestly exempts us from having to adopt this point of view which, though legitimate enough for theology or for other sciences or particular speculations, has nothing metaphysical about it. Fundamentally, the existence of extra-human, or supra-human, beings, which may assuredly include an indefinitude of types, is of little importance to us, whatever may be the names by which they are designated; even if we have every reason to admit their existence, since we see non-human beings in the world around us and consequently conclude that in other states there must be beings that do not pass through human manifestation (even if it be only those that are represented here by these non-human individualities), we nevertheless have no motive for occupying ourselves especially with them, any more than with the infra-human beings, which also exist and could be envisaged in the same fashion. No one would dream of making the detailed classification of the non-human beings of the terrestrial world the subject of a metaphysical study, or one so called; why then should it be otherwise for beings that happen to exist in other worlds, that is, that occupy other states, which, however superior they may be in relation to our own, are nonetheless,

and by the same token, part of the domain of universal manifestation? It is easy to see that those philosophers who wished to limit the
being to a single state, considering man in his more or less extended
individuality as constituting a complete whole unto himself,
although led nevertheless for some reason to postulate vaguely that
there are other degrees within universal Existence, have only con-
strued these degrees as the domains of beings that are completely
alien to us, except in what they have in common with all beings;
and, at the same time, an anthropomorphic tendency has often
inclined them to exaggerate such a commonality of nature by attributing to these beings faculties not simply analogous, but similar or
even identical, to those belonging properly to individual man.[1] In
reality, the states concerned are incomparably more different from
the human state than any modern Western philosopher has ever
been able to conceive even remotely; nonetheless, whatever the
beings currently occupying them, these states can equally well be
realized by all other beings, including a being that is simultaneously
a human being in another state of manifestation, for otherwise, as
we have already said, there could not be any question of the totality
of any being, since to be effective, that totality must necessarily
include all states both of manifestation (formal and non-formal) as
well as of non-manifestation, each according to the mode in which
the being under consideration is capable of realizing it. We have
noted elsewhere that nearly all that has been said theologically of the
angels can be said metaphysically of the superior states of the
being,[2] just as in the astrological symbolism of the Middle Ages the
'heavens', that is to say the various planetary and stellar spheres, represent these same states and also the initiatic degrees to which their
realization corresponds;[3] and like the 'heavens' and 'hells', the *Devas*

---

1. If the 'angelic' states are the supra-individual states constituting non-formal
manifestation, one cannot then attribute to the angels any of the faculties that are
properly of an individual order. For example, as we have said above, one cannot
suppose them endowed with reason, which is the exclusive characteristic of the
human individuality, for their mode of intelligence can only be purely intuitive.

2. *Man and His Becoming*, chap. 10. The treatise 'De Angelis' of Saint Thomas
Aquinas is particularly characteristic in this regard.

3. *The Esoterism of Dante*, chaps. 2 and 7.

and *Asuras* in the Hindu tradition, represent respectively the superior and inferior states in relation to the human state.[4] All this does
not of course exclude any modes of realization that may be proper
to other beings, just as there are modes peculiar to the human being
to the extent that his individual state is taken as a starting-point and
as a basis for realization; but these modes that are foreign to us are
no more important to us than are all the forms that we will never be
called upon to realize, such as the animal, vegetable, and mineral
forms of the corporeal world, because they are already realized by
other beings in the order of universal manifestation, of which the
indefinitude excludes all repetition.[5]

It follows from what we have just said that by 'spiritual hierarchies' we cannot properly mean anything other than the totality of
the states of being that are superior to human individuality, and
more especially of the non-formal or supra-individual states, states
that we must regard as realizable for the being starting from the
human state, even in the course of its corporeal and terrestrial existence. This realization is essentially implied in the totalization of the
being, and thus in the 'Deliverance' (*Moksha* or *Mukti*) by which the
being is freed from the ties of every special condition of existence,
and which, not being susceptible of differing degrees, is as complete
and perfect when it is obtained as 'liberation in life' (*jīvan-mukti*) as
it is in the case of 'liberation beyond form' (*videha-mukti*), as we
have already set forth elsewhere.[6] Moreover there can be no spiritual
degree superior to that of the *Yogi*, for the latter, having attained that
'Deliverance' which is at the same time 'Union' (*Yoga*) or 'Supreme
Identity', has nothing further to attain; but though the goal to be
reached is the same for all beings, each, of course, must reach it
according to its 'personal way', and hence by modalities susceptible
of indefinite variations. One will understand therefore that in the
course of this realization there may be multiple and various stages,
which, moreover, may be traversed successively or simultaneously
as the case may be, and which, since they still refer to determinate

4. *The Symbolism of the Cross*, chap. 25.
5. Cf. ibid., chap. 15.
6. *Man and His Becoming*, chap. 23.

states, must never be confused with the total liberation that is their supreme outcome and conclusion;[7] and here we have just as many degrees as can be envisaged in the 'spiritual hierarchies', whatever more or less general classification one establishes according to need, in the indefinitude of their possible modalities, the classification naturally depending on the particular point of view one chooses to adopt.[8]

At this point it is essential to note that the degrees of which we speak, representing as they do states that are still contingent and conditioned, are of no metaphysical importance in themselves but are so only in view of the unique goal to which they all tend, and precisely to the extent that they are regarded as degrees; of this goal they merely constitute a sort of preparation. Moreover, there is no common measure between any particular state, however elevated, and the total and unconditioned state; and one must never lose sight of the fact that since from the standpoint of the Infinite the entirety of manifestation is strictly nil, the differences between its component states must obviously be so as well, however consider-able these differences may be in themselves when one envisages only the various conditioned states separating them from each other. If the passage to certain superior states in some way constitutes a progress toward 'Deliverance' relative to the state taken as a point of departure, it must nevertheless be understood that when the latter is realized, it will always imply a discontinuity with respect to the immediately preceding state of the being that achieves it, and that the discontinuity will be neither more nor less profound whatever this state may be, since in all cases there is between the 'undelivered' and the 'delivered' being no relation such as exists between the dif-ferent conditioned states.[9]

---

7. Cf. ibid., chaps. 21 and 22.

8. These 'spiritual hierarchies', insofar as the various states they comprise are realized by the attainment of as many effective initiatic degrees, correspond to what Islamic esoterism calls the 'categories of initiation' (*Tartīb at-taṣawwuf*); on this subject we draw attention especially to the treatise of the same name written by Muḥyi 'd-Dīn ibn al-'Arabī.

9. See *Man and His Becoming*, chap. 20.

By reason of the equivalence of all the states *vis-à-vis* the Absolute, when the final goal is attained from any degree the being need not previously have traversed all other degrees since thenceforward it already possesses them all into the bargain, so to speak, because they are integral elements of its totalization. On the other hand, when there is reason to do so, the being that possesses all the states can obviously always be considered in relation to one of these states more particularly, and as if 'situated' effectively therein, although in reality it is beyond all states, and, so far from being contained in any of them, contains them all within itself. One could say that in such a case the states will simply be various aspects constituting as many 'functions' of the being, without its being at all affected by their conditions, conditions that exist for it only in illusory mode, since, insofar as it is truly the 'Self', its state is essentially unconditioned. It is thus that its appearance in respect of form, even its corporeal appearance, can subsist for a being that is 'delivered in life' (*jīvan-mukta*), and that 'during its residence in the body it is not affected by its properties, just as the sky is not affected by what floats upon its bosom';[10] and it remains equally 'unaffected' by all other contingencies, whatever the state, individual or supra-individual, that is, formal or non-formal, to which they refer in the order of manifestation, which in the final analysis is only itself the sum of all contingencies.

10. From Shankarāchārya, *Ātmā-Bodha* (see ibid., *Man and His Becoming*, chap. 23).

14

REPLY TO OBJECTIONS DRAWN FROM THE PLURALITY OF BEINGS

THERE is one point in the preceding that might still lend itself to an objection, although in truth we have already answered it in part, at least implicitly, in what we just said regarding the 'spiritual hierarchies'. The objection runs as follows: given that there exists an indefinitude of modalities realized by different beings, is it really legitimate to speak of totality in the case of each being? One can reply first of all by pointing out that the objection thus phrased obviously applies only to the manifested states, since in non-manifestation there can be no question of any kind of real distinction, so that from the standpoint of these non-manifested states what belongs to one being belongs equally to all insofar as they have effectively realized these states. Now, if one considers the totality of manifestation from this same standpoint, it constitutes only a simple 'accident' in the proper sense of the word by reason of its contingency, so that the importance of any one of its modalities considered in itself and 'distinctively' is then strictly nil. Furthermore, since in principle non-manifestation contains all that constitutes the profound and essential reality of things existing in any mode of manifestation, i.e., that without which the manifested would have only a purely illusory existence, one can say that the being that has effectively attained the state of non-manifestation thereby possesses all other states 'into the bargain' in the same way that it possesses all the intermediary states or degrees, even without having specifically passed through them previously, as we said in the last chapter.

This answer, which considers only the being that has reached total realization, is fully sufficient from the purely metaphysical point of view, and indeed is the only answer that can really suffice, for if we did not view the being in this way, that is, if we took any position other than this, there would no longer be reason to speak of totality, and the objection itself would no longer apply. In short, what needs to be said both here and in response to objections concerning the existence of multiplicity, is that manifestation considered as such, that is, under the aspect of the distinctions that condition it, is nothing with respect to non-manifestation, for there can be no common measure between the one and the other; what is absolutely real (all the rest being only illusory, in the sense of a reality that is merely derivative and, as it were, 'participated'), even for the possibilities comprising manifestation, is the permanent and unconditioned state under which they belong principially and fundamentally to the order of non-manifestation.

Although the above should be sufficient, let us turn now to yet another aspect of the question, and consider the being as having realized, not the totality of the unconditioned Self, but only the integrality of a certain state. In this case, the preceding objection must take a new form: how is it possible to envisage this integrality for a single being, when the state in question constitutes a domain common to an indefinitude of other beings insofar as the latter are equally subject to the conditions that characterize and determine this state or mode of existence? This objection is not the same but, with all due proportion being kept between the two cases, only analogous, and so the answer must also be analogous; for the being that is effectively placed at the central point of view of the state under consideration (which is the only possible way of realizing the integrality of the state), all other more or less particular points of view, insofar as they are taken distinctively, are no longer important, since they are then unified in this central point of view; thus they henceforth exist for the being in the unity of the latter, and they no longer exist outside of this unity, for the existence of multiplicity outside of unity is purely illusory. The being that has realized the integrality of a state has itself become the center of that state, and, this being the case, one may say that it fills this state entirely with its own irradiation;[1] it assimilates to itself all that is contained therein, making of it so many secondary modalities of itself,[2] as it were, comparable somewhat to the modalities that are realized in the dream state, following what we said above. Consequently, the being is not in the least affected in its extension by the existence that these modalities, or at least some of them, can otherwise have outside of itself (and the expression 'outside' no longer has any meaning from the point of view of the being, but only from that of other beings remaining in non-unified multiplicity) by reason of the simultaneous existence of other beings in the same state; moreover, the existence of these same modalities in and of itself in no way affects its unity, even when it is still only a question of the relative unity realized at the center of a particular state. The whole of that state is constituted only by the irradiation of its center,[3] and any being effectively positioned at this center by that very fact becomes master of the state in its integrality; thus the principial indifferentiation of the non-manifested is reflected in the manifested, it being clearly understood that the reflection retains the relativity inherent in all conditioned existence, since it is in the manifested realm.

Having established this much, it is easy to understand that in various ways analogous considerations can be applied to the modalities included in an even more relative unity, such as that of a being that has only realized a certain state partially, and not integrally. Such a being, the human individual for example, without having yet achieved its full development in the sense of 'amplitude' (corresponding to the degree of existence in which it is situated), has still however assimilated more or less completely all of which it has truly become conscious within the limits of its present extension; and the accessory modalities that it has thus taken on, and that are obviously susceptible of constant and indefinite growth, constitute a very important part of those prolongations of the individuality to which we have already frequently alluded.

---

1. Cf. *Man and His Becoming*, chap. 16.
2. The symbolism of nourishment (*anna*) is frequently used in the Upanishads to designate this kind of assimilation.
3. This has been explained amply in *The Symbolism of the Cross*.

15

THE REALIZATION
OF THE BEING THROUGH
KNOWLEDGE

WE HAVE JUST SAID THAT THE BEING assimilates more or less completely everything of which it is conscious; indeed, there is no true knowledge in any domain whatsoever, other than that which enables us to penetrate into the intimate nature of things, and the degrees of knowledge consist precisely in the measure to which this penetration is more or less profound and results in a more or less complete assimilation. In other words, the only genuine knowledge is that which implies an identification of the subject with the object, or, if one prefers to consider the relationship inversely, an assimilation of the object by the subject,[1] and consequently the measure to which such an identification or such an assimilation is actually implied constitutes precisely the degrees of knowledge themselves.[2] We must therefore maintain, despite all the more or less idle philosophical discussions that this point has given

---

1. It should be clearly understood that here we take the terms 'subject' and 'object' in their usual sense, as designating respectively 'the one who knows' and 'that which is known' (see *Man and His Becoming*, chap. 15).

2. We have already mentioned on various occasions that in principle Aristotle posited identification by knowledge, but also that this affirmation, in his works as in those of his Scholastic followers, seems to have remained purely theoretical, for they seem never to have drawn any conclusions from it as concerns metaphysical realization (see especially *Introduction to the Study of the Hindu Doctrines*, pt. 2, chap. 10; and *Man and His Becoming*, chap. 24).

rise to,[3] that all true and effective knowledge is immediate, and that mediate knowledge can have only a purely symbolic and representative value.[4] As for the actual possibility of immediate knowledge, the whole theory of multiple states makes it sufficiently comprehensible. Besides, to wish to cast doubt upon it is merely to give proof of complete ignorance of the most elementary metaphysical principles, since without this immediate knowledge, metaphysics itself would be impossible.[5]

We have spoken of identification or assimilation, and we can employ these two terms almost indifferently here, although they do not arise from exactly the same point of view; in the same way, one can regard knowledge as proceeding simultaneously from the subject to the object of which it becomes conscious (or, more generally, and in order not to limit ourselves to the conditions of certain states, from which it makes a secondary modality of itself), and from the object to the subject that assimilates it to itself; and in this context it is worth recalling the Aristotelian definition of knowledge in the sensible domain as 'the common act of perceiver and perceived,' which in effect implies such a reciprocity of relationship.[6] Where the sensible and corporeal domain is concerned, the sense organs are thus the 'entryways' of knowledge for the individual being;[7] but from another point of view they are also precisely the 'outlets' in that all knowledge implies an act of identification starting from the knowing subject and proceeding toward the known (or to be known) object, like the emission of a sort of exterior prolongation of itself. And it is important to note that such a prolongation

---

3. We allude here to the modern 'theories of knowledge', whose futility we have already explained elsewhere (*Introduction to the Study of the Hindu Doctrines*, pt. 2, chap. 10), a point to which we shall shortly return.

4. This difference is that between intuitive and discursive knowledge, about which we have already spoken so often that we need not linger over it here.

5. See *Introduction to the Study of the Hindu Doctrines*, pt. 2, chap. 5.

6. One might note also that the act common to two beings, following the sense which Aristotle gives to the word 'act', is that by which their natures coincide, and are thus identified, at least partially.

7. See *Man and His Becoming*, chap. 12. The symbolism of the 'mouths' of *Vaishvānara* is related to the analogy of cognitive with nutritive assimilation.

is only exterior in relation to the individuality envisaged in its most restricted sense, for it is an integral part of the extended individuality; in extending itself thus by a development of its own possibilities, the being has no need at all to go outside of itself, which, in reality, would make no sense since under no conditions can a being become other than itself. This is also a direct response to the principal objection of modern Western philosophers against the possibility of immediate knowledge, from which it is evident that this objection could only arise from a pure and simple metaphysical incomprehension, in consequence of which these philosophers have failed to recognize the possibilities of being, even individual being, in its indefinite extension.

All this is true *a fortiori* if, leaving behind the limits of the individuality, we apply it to superior states; true knowledge of these states implies their effective possession, and, inversely, it is by this very knowledge that the being takes possession of them, for the two acts are inseparable one from another, and we could even say that fundamentally they are but one. Naturally, this must be understood only of immediate knowledge, which, when it extends to the totality of states, includes in itself their realization, and which, consequently, is 'the only means of obtaining complete and final Deliverance.'[8] As for knowledge that has remained purely theoretical, it is obvious that it could in no way be equivalent to such a realization, and that, not being an immediate seizure of its object, it can only have an altogether symbolic value, as we have already said; but it nonetheless constitutes an indispensable preparation for the acquisition of that effective knowledge whereby, and whereby alone, the realization of the total being takes place.

Whenever occasion arises, we must insist particularly upon the realization of the being through knowledge, because it is altogether foreign to modern Western conceptions, which do not go beyond theoretical knowledge, or, more exactly, beyond a slender portion of it, and which artificially oppose 'knowledge' to 'being' as if they were not the two inseparable faces of one and the same reality.[9]

---

8. Shankarāchārya, *Ātmā-Bodha* (ibid., chap. 22).
9. See also *Introduction to the Study of the Hindu Doctrines*, pt. 2, chap. 10.

There can be no true metaphysics for anyone who does not truly understand that the being realizes itself through knowledge, and that it can only realize itself in this way. Pure metaphysical doctrine does not need to trouble itself in the least with all the 'theories of knowledge' that modern philosophy so laboriously elaborates; in these efforts to substitute a 'theory of knowledge' for knowledge itself one can even see a veritable admission of impotence, albeit certainly unconscious, on the part of this philosophy, so completely ignorant is it of any possibility of effective realization. What is more, true knowledge being immediate as we have said, can be more or less complete, more or less profound, more or less adequate, but it cannot be essentially 'relative', as this same philosophy would have it, or at least it could be so only insofar as its objects are themselves relative. In other words, relative knowledge, metaphysically speaking, is nothing but knowledge of the relative or of the contingent, that is to say of what applies only to the realm of manifestation; but the validity of this knowledge within its own domain is only as great as the nature of the domain allows,[10] which is not what is meant by those who speak of the 'relativity of knowledge'. Apart from consideration of the degrees of a more or less complete and profound knowledge—degrees that change nothing of its essential nature—the only legitimate distinction to be made as to the validity of knowledge is the distinction we have already noted between immediate and mediate knowledge, that is, between effective and symbolic knowledge.

10. This applies even to simple sensible knowledge, which in its own inferior and limited order is also immediate, and thus necessarily true.

16

KNOWLEDGE
AND CONSCIOUSNESS

A VERY IMPORTANT CONSEQUENCE of the foregoing is that knowledge, understood absolutely and in all its universality, is in no way synonymous with or equivalent to consciousness, whose domain is coextensive only with that of certain determined states of being, so that it is only in those states to the exclusion of all others, that knowledge is realized by means of what can properly be called 'becoming conscious' of anything. Consciousness, as we have understood the term until now, even in its most general sense and without restricting it to its specifically human form, is only a contingent and special mode of knowledge under certain conditions, a property inherent to a being envisaged in certain states of manifestation; all the more reason, then, to say that it is not applicable in any degree to unconditioned states, that is, to all that goes beyond Being, since it is not even applicable to the whole of Being. Knowledge, on the contrary, considered in itself and independently of the conditions attaching to any particular state, can admit of no restriction, and to be adequate to total truth must be coextensive not only with Being but also with universal Possibility itself, and therefore it must be infinite, as the latter necessarily is. This amounts to saying that knowledge and truth, envisaged thus metaphysically, are basically nothing other than what we have called rather inadequately 'aspects of the Infinite'; this is something clearly expressed in one of the fundamental formulations of the *Vedānta*: '*Brahma* is Truth, Knowledge, Infinity' (*Satyam Jnānam Anantam Brahma*).[1]

---

1. *Taittirīya Upanishad*, II.1.1.

When we say that 'knowing' and 'being' are the two faces of a single reality, the term 'being' should be taken only in its analogical and symbolic sense, since knowledge goes further than Being; here, as when we speak of the realization of the total being, realization, which essentially implies total and absolute knowledge, is in no way distinct from that knowledge itself (of course insofar as the knowledge is effective and not merely theoretical and representative). At this point we should also clarify somewhat how the metaphysical identity of the possible and the real should be understood. Since everything possible is realized by knowledge, this identity, taken universally, properly constitutes truth in itself, for the latter can be conceived precisely as the perfect adequation of knowledge to total Possibility.[2] It is easy to see all the consequences that might be drawn from this last remark, the implications of which are immensely greater in extent than those of a simply logical definition of truth, for here we have all the difference between the universal unconditioned intellect[3] and human understanding with its individual conditions, and also, in another respect, all the difference separating the point of view of realization from that of a 'theory of knowledge'. The very word 'real', usually so vague and even equivocal, especially for the philosophers who maintain the so-called distinction between the possible and the real, takes on an altogether different metaphysical value when used in reference to realization,[4] or, to be more precise, on becoming an expression of absolute permanence, in the Universal, of all that of which a being attains effective possession by the total realization of itself.[5]

---

2. This formula accords with the definition Saint Thomas Aquinas gives of truth as *adaequatio rei et intellectus*; but it is a kind of transposition as it were, for it is necessary to take into account the principal difference that Scholastic doctrine is limited exclusively to Being, whereas what we have been saying here applies equally to all that is beyond Being.

3. Here the term 'intellect' is also transposed beyond Being, and thus all the more so beyond *Buddhi*, which though of a universal and non-formal order still belongs to the domain of manifestation, and consequently cannot be called unconditioned.

4. One will note moreover the far from fortuitous close relation between the words 'real' and 'realization'.

5. It is this same permanence that Western theology expresses in another way when it says that all possibles are eternally in the divine understanding.

The intellect as universal principle could be conceived as the container of total knowledge, but on condition that this be seen only as a simple figure of speech, for here, where we are essentially at the level of 'non-duality', the container and the contained are absolutely identical, both being of necessity equally infinite—a 'plurality of infinities', as we have said before, being an impossibility. Universal Possibility, which contains all, cannot be contained by anything, unless it be by itself, and it contains itself 'without this containing existing in any way whatsoever.'[6] Moreover, intellect and knowledge can only be spoken of correlatively in the universal sense, in the way the Infinite and Possibility were discussed above, that is to say viewed as one and the same thing, which we envisaged simultaneously under an active and a passive aspect, but without there being any real distinction. In the Universal we should not distinguish intellect from knowledge, nor, in consequence, the intelligible from the knowable; true knowledge being immediate, the intellect is strictly speaking but one with its object; it is only in conditioned modes of knowledge, which are always indirect and inadequate, that there is reason to establish a distinction, since this relative knowledge then operates not by the intellect itself but by a refraction of the intellect in the states of being concerned, and, as we have seen, it is just such a refraction that constitutes individual consciousness; but, directly or indirectly, there is always participation in the universal intellect in the measure in which there is effective knowledge, whether in any mode whatsoever or outside of every particular mode.

Since total knowledge is adequate to universal Possibility, there is nothing that is unknowable,[7] or, in other words, 'there are no incomprehensible things, there are only things incomprehensible at

---

6. Muḥyi 'd-Dīn ibn al-'Arabī, *Risālat-al-Ahadiya* (see *Man and His Becoming*, chap. 15).

7. Therefore we reject formally and absolutely all 'agnosticism', of any degree whatsoever; besides, if one were to ask the 'positivists', as well as the partisans of Herbert Spencer's famous theory of the 'unknowable', by what authority they affirm that there are things which cannot be known, the question would run a good risk of remaining unanswered, the more so because some of them seem quite simply to confuse the 'unknown' (that is, what is unknown to themselves), with the 'unknowable' (see *East and West*, pt. 1, chap. 1, and *The Crisis of the Modern World*, chap. 5).

present,'[8] things inconceivable, not in themselves and absolutely, but only to us as conditioned beings, that is, as beings limited in our present manifestation to the possibilities of a determinate state. We thus set forth what could be called a principle of 'universal intelligibility', not as this is ordinarily understood, however, but in a purely metaphysical sense, and hence beyond the logical domain in which this principle, like all those of a properly universal order (which alone truly deserve to be called 'principles'), find only a particular and contingent application. For us, of course, this postulates no 'rationalism', quite the contrary, since reason, differing essentially from intellect, without whose guarantee it could not in any case be valid, is nothing more than a specifically human and individual faculty. There is thus necessarily, we do not say the 'irrational',[9] but the 'supra-rational', which, in fact, is a fundamental characteristic of everything of a truly metaphysical order; and this 'supra-rational' does not for all that cease to be intelligible in itself, even if it is not at present comprehensible to the limited and relative faculties of human individuality.[10]

This suggests yet another observation well worth considering in order to avoid any error: like the word 'reason', the word 'consciousness' can sometimes be universalized by a purely analogical transposition, something we ourselves have done elsewhere to render the meaning of the Sanskrit word *Chit*;[11] but such a transposition is only possible when one restricts oneself to Being, as was done when the ternary *Satchidānanda* was under consideration. It should be strictly understood, however, that even with this restriction, consciousness thus transposed is no longer understood in its proper sense, such as we have defined it above, and as we have generally taken it. In this usual sense, let us repeat, consciousness is only the

---

8. Matgioi, *La Voie Metaphysique*, third edition, p73.

9. That which surpasses reason is not by that fact contrary to reason, which is what is generally understood by the word 'irrational'.

10. Let us recall in this connection that a 'mystery', even understood theologically, is not at all something unknowable or unintelligible, but rather, taken in its etymological sense, something inexpressible and so incommunicable, which is an altogether different matter.

11. *Man and His Becoming*, chap. 14.

special mode of a contingent and relative knowledge, as relative and contingent as the conditioned state of being to which it essentially belongs; and, if one can say that it is a 'raison d' être' for such a state, it is so only insofar as it is a participation by refraction in the nature of that universal and transcendent intellect that is itself, finally and eminently, the supreme 'raison d' être' of all things, the true metaphysical 'sufficient reason' that determines itself in all the orders of possibilities, without these determinations being able to affect it in any way whatsoever. This conception of 'sufficient reason', very different from the philosophical or theological conceptions in which Western thought is imprisoned, immediately resolves many questions before which the latter must confess itself impotent, by bringing about a reconciliation between the point of view of necessity and that of contingency. Here we are in fact well beyond the opposition of necessity and contingency understood in their ordinary acceptation,[12] and thus some complementary elucidation on this subject may perhaps not be without value in our effort to understand why the question need not arise in pure metaphysics.

12. Let us say, moreover, that theology, far superior in this respect to philosophy, at least recognizes that this opposition can and must be transcended, although here the resolution is not in such clear evidence as when it is envisaged from the metaphysical point of view. And it should be added that it is from the theological point of view above all, and by reason of the religious conception of 'creation', that this question of the relationships between necessity and contingency from the beginning took on the importance that it has henceforth retained philosophically in Western thought.

17

NECESSITY
AND CONTINGENCY

WE SAID EARLIEr that every possibility of manifestation must be manifested for the very reason that it is what it is, namely, a possibility of manifestation, so that manifestation is necessarily implied in principle by the very nature of particular possibilities. Thus manifestation, which as such is purely contingent, is nonetheless necessary in its principle, just as, although transitory in itself, it nevertheless possesses an absolutely permanent root in universal Possibility, this moreover being what constitutes all its reality. If it were otherwise, manifestation could only have an altogether illusory existence, which could even be regarded as strictly non-existent, since, being without principle, it would retain only an essentially 'privative' character, like that of a negation or a limitation considered in itself; and envisaged in this way, manifestation would in effect be nothing more than the totality of all possible limiting conditions. However, from the moment these conditions are possible, they are metaphysically real, and this reality, which was only negative when the conditions were conceived as simple limitations, becomes in a way positive when they are envisaged as possibilities. It is thus because manifestation is implied in the order of possibilities that it has its proper reality, though without this reality being in any way capable of existence independent of the universal order, for it is there, and there alone, that it has its true 'sufficient reason': to say that manifestation is necessary in principle is basically nothing else than to say that it is contained in universal Possibility.

There is no difficulty in conceiving that manifestation may thus be at once necessary and contingent from different points of view, provided one pays careful attention to the fundamental point that the principle cannot be affected by any determination whatsoever, since it is essentially independent of them all, as the cause is independent of its effects, so that manifestation, necessitated by its principle, cannot inversely necessitate the latter in any way. It is therefore the 'irreversibility' or 'irreciprocity' of the relationship as here envisaged that resolves the entire difficulty usually supposed to vex this question,[1] a difficulty that really only exists when this 'irreciprocity' is lost sight of; and if one loses sight of it (supposing one has ever had it in view to any degree), it is because, being situated currently in manifestation, one is naturally led to attribute to this an importance that it could never have from the universal point of view. To make this more comprehensible, let us again take a spatial symbol, and say that in its integrality manifestation is truly nil with respect to the Infinite, just as, allowing for the reservations that the imperfection of such comparisons always requires, a point situated in space is equal to zero with respect to that space.[2] This does not mean that the point is absolutely nothing, the more so as it necessarily exists by the very fact that space exists, but rather that it is nothing in relation to extension, as it is strictly a zero of extension; and in relation to the universal All, manifestation is nothing more than what this point is in relation to space envisaged in all the indefinitude of its extension, but with the difference that space is something limited by its own nature, whereas the universal All is the Infinite.

Here we should mention another difficulty, but one that consists much more in the expression than in the conception itself: all that exists in a transitory mode in manifestation must be transposed into a permanent mode in the non-manifested; manifestation itself thus acquires the permanence that constitutes all its principial reality, but it is then no longer manifestation as such, but rather the ensemble of the possibilities of manifestation insofar as they are not manifested, while nonetheless still implying manifestation in their own

1. It is this very 'irreciprocity' that equally excludes all 'pantheism' and all 'immanentism', as we have pointed out elsewhere (*Man and His Becoming*, chap. 24).

2. It is a case here, of course, of a point located in space, and not the principial point, of which space itself is only an expansion or a development. On the relations between point and extension see *The Symbolism of the Cross*, chap. 16.

nature (without which they would be other than what they are). The difficulty of this transposition or this passage from the manifested to the non-manifested, and the apparent obscurity that results, is the same as is encountered in trying to express, in the measure that they are expressible, the relations between time (or more generally duration in all its modes, that is to say, the whole condition of successive existence) and eternity. This is essentially the same question envisaged under two scarcely distinguishable aspects, of which the second is simply more particular than the first since it refers only to one determined condition among all those comprised in the manifested. All of this, we repeat, is perfectly conceivable, but one must be able to take the inexpressible into consideration, as is required in all that pertains to the metaphysical domain; as concerns the means of realization of an effective, as opposed to a merely theoretical, conception that extends even to the inexpressible, we obviously cannot speak of it in this study, considerations of this order not entering into the framework of the task we have set ourselves at present.

Returning to contingency, we may define it in a general way as that which does not contain in itself its own sufficient reason; but even so it is evident that every contingent thing is nonetheless necessary in the sense that it is necessitated by its sufficient reason, which it must have in order to exist, even if it does not lie within it, at least when envisaged under the special conditions in which it has precisely this character of contingency; and it would no longer have this character if envisaged in its principle, since it would then be identified with its sufficient reason itself. Such is the case of manifestation, which as such is contingent because its principle or its sufficient reason is to be found in the non-manifested insofar as the latter includes what we may call the 'manifestable', that is to say the possibilities of manifestation as pure possibilities, and not, it goes without saying, insofar as it includes the 'non-manifestable', or the possibilities of non-manifestation. Principle and sufficient reason are thus fundamentally the same thing, but if one wishes to understand the idea of contingency in its metaphysical sense, it is particularly important to consider the principle under this aspect of sufficient reason; and to avoid all confusion it should again be made clear that the sufficient reason is exclusively the final raison d'être of a thing (final if one leaves the consideration of the thing in order to ascend to the principle, but in reality, primary in the order of sequence, logical as well as ontological, which leads from the principle to its consequences) and not simply its immediate raison d'être, for everything that is in any mode whatsoever, even a contingent one, must have in itself its immediate raison d'être, understood in the sense employed previously when we said that consciousness constitutes a raison d'être for certain states of manifested existence.

A most important consequence of this is that one can say that every being bears its destiny within itself, whether in a relative fashion (individual destiny), if it is merely a case of the being envisaged within a certain conditioned state, or in an absolute fashion, if it is a case of the being in its totality, since 'the word "destiny" designates the true reason of things.'[3] The conditioned or relative being can only bear in itself an equally relative destiny, however, relating exclusively to its special conditions of existence; if, considering a being in this way, one wished to speak of its final or absolute destiny, this latter would no longer be within it, but that is because it is in truth no longer the destiny of this contingent being as such, since it refers in reality to the total being. This observation should suffice to demonstrate the inanity of all discussion on the topic of 'determinism',[4] this being another of those questions so numerous in modern Western philosophy that only exist because they are wrongly posed; moreover there are so many different conceptions of determinism, and just as many of freedom, most of which have nothing at all metaphysical about them, that it is important to define the true metaphysical notion of freedom, the subject with which we propose to conclude this study.

---

3. Traditional commentary of Chuang Tzu on the *I Ching* (cf. *The Symbolism of the Cross*, chap. 22).

4. One could say as much of the better part of the discussions relating to finality, the distinction between 'internal finality' and 'external finality' being valid only insofar as one admits the anti-metaphysical supposition that an individual being is a complete being and constitutes a 'closed system', since otherwise that which is 'external' for the individual can nonetheless be 'internal' for the true being, if indeed the distinction presupposed by the word is still applicable (see *The Symbolism of the Cross*, chap. 29); and it is easy to see that in the end finality and destiny are identical.

18

THE METAPHYSICAL
NOTION OF FREEDOM

To PROVE FREEDOM METAPHYSICALLY, without encumbering oneself with all the usual philosophical arguments, it is sufficient to establish that it is a possibility, since the possible and the real are metaphysically identical. To this end we may first define freedom as the absence of constraint, a definition negative in form but, here again, fundamentally positive, for it is constraint that is a limitation, that is to say a veritable negation. Now, as we said above, when one envisages universal Possibility beyond Being, that is, as Non-Being, one cannot speak of unity, since Non-Being is metaphysical Zero, but at least one can speak of 'non-duality' (*advaita*),[1] to continue to use a negative form. Where there is no duality, there is necessarily no constraint, and this suffices to prove that freedom is a possibility insofar as it results immediately from 'non-duality', which is obviously exempt from every contradiction.

Now, one can add also that freedom is not only a possibility in the most universal sense, but also a possibility of being or of manifestation; here, in order to pass from Non-Being to Being, it suffices to pass from 'non-duality' to unity: Being is 'one' (the One being Zero affirmed), or, rather, it is metaphysical Unity itself—the first affirmation, but also by that very token the first determination.[2] That which is one is manifestly exempt from all constraint, so that the absence of constraint, that is, freedom, is again in the domain of Being, where unity presents itself in a way as a specification of the

1. Cf. *Man and His Becoming*, chap. 22.
2. Ibid., chap. 6.

principial 'non-duality' of Non-Being; in other words, freedom also belongs to Being, which amounts to saying that it is a possibility of being, or, following our previous explanations, a possibility of manifestation, since Being is pre-eminently the principle of manifestation. Furthermore, to say that this possibility is essentially inherent in Being as an immediate consequence of its unity is to say that it will be manifested in some degree, in all that proceeds from Being, that is to say in all particular beings insofar as they belong to the domain of universal manifestation. However, as soon as there is multiplicity, as is the case in the order of particular existences, it is evident that there can no longer be a question of any but relative freedom; and in this respect one may envisage either the multiplicity of particular beings themselves or that of the elements constituting each one of them. As concerns the multiplicity of beings, each is limited by the others in its states of manifestation, and this limitation can be expressed as a restriction on its freedom; but to say that some being is not free to any degree would be to say that it is not itself, that it is 'the others', or that it does not bear even its immediate raison d'être within itself, which would amount to saying that it is in no way a real being.[3] Furthermore, since the unity of Being is the principle of freedom in particular beings as well as in universal Being, a being will be free to the extent that it participates in this unity; in other words, it will be the more free as it has more unity in itself, or as it is more 'one';[4] but, as we have already said, individual beings are never such except in a relative way.[5] In this regard moreover it is important to note that it is not exactly the greater or lesser

3. One might also add that, since multiplicity proceeds from the unity in which it is implied or contained in principle, it cannot in any way destroy either unity or any consequences of unity, such as freedom.

4. Every being, to truly be such, must have a certain unity the principle of which it carries in itself; in this sense Leibnitz was right in saying: 'That which is not truly *a* being is not a *being* at all.' But this adaptation of the Scholastic formula *ens et unum convertuntur* loses for him its metaphysical importance by its attribution of absolute and complete unity to 'individual substances'.

5. It is moreover by reason of this relativity that one may speak of degrees of unity, and hence of degrees of freedom, for there are degrees only in the relative, the absolute not being susceptible of any 'more' or 'less' (taking these words here analogically, not merely in their quantitative sense).

complexity of the constitution of the being that makes it more or less free, but it is rather the character of that complexity that determines to what degree it is more or less effectively unified, and this follows from what we have explained previously regarding the relationships between unity and multiplicity.[6]

Freedom thus envisaged is then a possibility which, to varying degrees, is an attribute of all beings, whatever they are and in whatever state they are situated, and not only of man; thus human freedom, which is all that is considered in philosophical discussions, no longer appears as anything but the particular case that it really is.[7] What matters most metaphysically is not the relative freedom of manifested beings, any more than the special and limited domains in which it may be exercised, but freedom understood in the universal sense, which properly resides in the metaphysical instant of passage from cause to effect, the causal relation moreover having to be transposed analogically in such a way as to be applicable to all

---

6. It is necessary to distinguish between that complexity which is only pure multiplicity and that which, on the contrary, is an expansion of unity (cf. *asrār rabbāniyyah* in Islamic esoterism; *Man and His Becoming*, chap. 9, and *The Symbolism of the Cross*, chap. 4); one could say that in relation to the possibilities of Being, the former refers to 'substance' and the latter to 'essence.'

One could similarly envisage the relations of one being with others (relations which, considered in the state where they occur, enter as elements into the complexity of its nature, since they make up part of its attributes as so many secondary modalities of itself) under two apparently opposed but really complementary aspects, according to whether in these relations the being in question assimilates the others to itself or is assimilated by them, that assimilation constituting 'comprehension' in the proper sense of the word. The relationship existing between two beings is at one and the same time a modification of both; but one can say that the determining cause of this modification lies in the one of the two beings which acts upon the other, or which assimilates it to itself when the relation is taken in the sense of the preceding point of view, a point of view which is no longer that of action but of knowledge insofar as it implies an identification between its two terms.

7. It matters little that some prefer to call 'spontaneity' what we here call freedom, in order to reserve the latter term especially for human freedom; but this usage of two different terms has the disadvantage of leading all too easily to the notion that the latter is of a different nature, whereas the difference is only one of degree, or that, at the very least, human freedom constitutes a kind of 'privileged case', which is metaphysically untenable.

orders of possibilities. Since this causal relation is not and cannot be one of succession, its accomplishment must be viewed here essentially under the extra-temporal aspect, and this all the more so in that the temporal point of view, being particular to a determined state of manifested existence, or, even more precisely, to certain modalities of that state, is in no way susceptible of universalization.[8] Consequently, this metaphysical instant, which seems so elusive because there is no break in continuity between the cause and the effect, is in reality unlimited, and thus, as we established at the outset, surpasses Being and is coextensive with total Possibility itself; it constitutes what one may call figuratively a 'state of universal consciousness',[9] participating in the 'permanent actuality' inherent in the 'first cause' itself.[10]

In Non-Being, the absence of constraint can only lie in 'non-action' (the *wu-wei* of the Far-Eastern tradition);[11] in Being, or, more exactly, in manifestation, freedom operates in differentiated activity, which in the individual human state takes the form of action in the usual sense of this word. Moreover, in the domain of action, and even in the whole of universal manifestation, the 'freedom of indifference' is impossible, since it is the mode of freedom belonging properly to the non-manifested (which, strictly speaking, is in no way a special mode),[12] that is to say, it is not freedom as a possibility of being, nor yet the freedom that belongs to Being (or to

---

8. Duration itself, understood in its most general sense as conditioning all existence in successive mode, that is to say as including every condition that in other states corresponds analogically to time, also cannot be universalized, since in the Universal everything must be envisaged in simultaneity.

9. Here one should recall what was said above concerning the reservations necessary when one wishes to universalize the sense of the word 'consciousness' by an analogical transposition. The expression used here is fundamentally a near equivalent to that of 'aspect of the Infinite', which also should not be taken literally.

10. Cf. Matgioi, *La Voie Metaphysique*, third edition, pp 73–74.

11. The 'Activity of Heaven' in itself (in the principial indifferentiation of Non-Being) is non-acting and non-manifested (see *The Symbolism of the Cross*, chap. 23).

12. It becomes so only in its ordinary philosophical conception, which is not merely erroneous but truly absurd, for it supposes that something could exist without having any raison d'être.

God conceived as Being in its relation to the world understood as the totality of universal manifestation) and consequently, to the manifested beings that occupy its domain and participate in its nature and attributes according to the measure of their own respective possibilities. The realization of the possibilities of manifestation which constitute all beings in all their manifested states, including all the modifications, whether of action or otherwise, that belong to these states, therefore cannot rest upon a pure indifference (or upon an arbitrary decree of the divine Will, after the well-known Cartesian theory that would moreover apply this conception of indifference both to God and to man),[13] but this realization is determined by the order of the universal possibility of manifestation, which is Being itself, so that Being determines itself, not only in itself (insofar as it is Being, the first of all determinations), but also in all its modalities, which are all the particular possibilities of manifestation. It is only in these latter, considered 'distinctively' and even under the aspect of 'separativity', that there can be determination by 'another than itself'; put another way, particular beings can both determine themselves (to the extent that each one of them possesses a certain unity, hence a certain freedom, as participating in Being) and be determined by other beings (by reason of the multiplicity of particular beings, which, insofar as they are envisaged from the point of view of the states of manifested existence, are not brought together into a unity). Universal Being cannot be determined, but determines itself; as for Non-Being, it can neither be determined nor determine itself, since, being beyond all determination, it admits of none.

One sees from the preceding that absolute freedom can be realized only through complete universalization; this will be 'self-determination' insofar as it is co-extensive with Being, and 'indetermination' beyond Being. Whereas a relative freedom belongs to every being under any condition whatsoever, this absolute freedom can only belong to the being that, liberated from the conditions of manifested existence, whether individual or even supra-individual,

---

13. We include the translation into theological terms here only to facilitate comparison with the customary points of view of Western thought.

has become absolutely 'one', at the degree of pure Being, or 'without duality', if its realization surpasses Being.[14] It is then, but then only, that one can speak of a being 'that is a law unto itself',[15] because this being is then entirely identical with its sufficient reason, which is both its principial origin and its final destiny.

14. See *Man and His Becoming*, chaps. 15 and 16.

15. Concerning this expression, which belongs more particularly to Islamic esoterism, and its equivalent *svēchchhāchāri* in Hindu doctrine, see *The Symbolism of the Cross*, chap. 9. See also what has been said on the state of the Yogi or *jīvan-mukta* in *Man and His Becoming*, chaps. 23 and 24.

INDEX

advaita 31, 90
agnosticism 83 n7
ahankāra 42, 48
Ākāsha 23
Alexandrian Gnosticism 25 n10
angelic states 49, 70 n1
angels 49, 70
Aristotle 67 n3, 77–78
Asuras 71
atomist(s) 18, 23

Being (defined) 20
Brahma 81
Brahmā 12 n13
Brahmānda ('World Egg'), 67 n7
Buddhi 42, 50, 52, 82 n3

Cartesian 'animal machines' 47
China 51 n7
Chuang Tzu 36–37, 89 n3

darshana 51
Descartes 18, 40 n10, 56 n5
determinism 89
Devas 70
Dragon, Far-Eastern symbolism
of 68 n10
dream state 35–36, 39, 41, 44, 76
dualism 56, 65
duality 32, 51, 90, 95

ens et unum convertuntur 91 n4
ens rationis 11 n10
ether 23
Euclidean geometry 14 n3

Fiat Lux 68

Greece 23 n5
Greek 24 n8
gunas 64

hallucination 38 n7
Hindu doctrine 12 n13, 29 n6, 31,
42, 95 n15
symbolism 67 n7
tradition 50 n4, 67 n8, 71
Hiranyagarbha 67 n7

immanentism 87 n1
India 23 n5, 51 n7
Islamic esoterism 28, 57 n1, 72
n8, 92 n6, 95 n15

jīvan-mukta 73, 95 n15
jīvan-mukti 71

Khien 12
Khouen 12
knowledge, Aristotelian
definition of 78

Leibnitz 14, 16–17, 38 n8, 91 n4
Logos, Platonic and Alexandrian
50

man, Aristotelian and Scholastic
definition of 48
manas 42, 48
Manu 50
māyāvi-rūpa 36

metaphysics 17 n7, 39, 42, 55, 69, 78, 80, 85
Moksha (Mukti) 71
Muḥyi'd Dīn ibn al-'Arabī 72 n8, 83 n6
multorum in uno expressio 38 n8

Nārāyana 67 n8
Non-Being 20–27, 31–32, 34, 65, 90–91, 93–94
non-duality 31, 83, 90–91

ontogeny 44
ontology 34

pantheism 10 n9, 87 n1
phylogeny 44
Pascal 32 n1
polypsychism 44
positivists 83 n7
psychologists 29 n10, 41–43, 52
psychology 18, 27, 41–42, 54 n1

rationalism 84
reincarnationist hypothesis 44

Saint Thomas Aquinas 70 n2, 82 n2
Satchidānanda 84
Scholastic doctrine 82 n2
    philosophers 11 n10, 50 n5

Shakti 12 n13
Shankarāchārya 73 n10, 79 n8
Spencer, Herbert 83 n7
subconscious 43
successive existences 44
superconscious 43
svechchhāchāri 95

tamas 68
Tao 37 n6
Taoist text 36
theology 69, 82 n5, 85 n12
transformism 44
transformist theories 45

universal Possibility 7, 9, 11–14, 17, 21, 44, 81, 83, 86, 90, 94
Upanishads 76 n2

Vaishvānara 78
Vedānta 81
videha-mukti 71
Vishnu 67 n8

Waḥdat al-wujūd 28
wu-wei 93

Yoga 71
Yogi 71, 95 n15

Zero, metaphysical 24, 31–33, 90

Printed in the United States
60760LVS00006B/73

9 780900 588594